# INDIGO FADING

## Casey Giles

Casey Giles
2020

ISBN (Softcover): 978-1-7334904-1-2





Visit the Author's website at
www.caseygiles.com

Ordering Information:
Quantity sales. Special discounts available for bulk purchases, sales promotions, fund-raising and educational needs, contact Sales Coordinator at
lilibeth4214@gmail.com

*For my friends.*

# Table of Contents

# An Untimely Death

My eyes snap open, trying to focus in the hazy lavender atmosphere. The sky crashes down on me in a blur. Thoughts and memories swirl around in my mind, but I can't make sense of any of them. There's a horrible burning sensation in my gut, and it feels like I've been shot, though I don't know why I'm familiar with what that feels like. The pain is almost too much to comprehend. I lift a trembling hand and brush the area with my fingers, only to recoil instantly as sparks shoot through my body and the taste of metal rises in my throat. My fingers are warm and sticky when they come away; they land inaudibly in what feels like water. Blinking in and out of consciousness, the white pain grounds my mind and keeps me from drifting off completely.

I heave in a ragged breath, and I'm reminded of the pain, but I try to ignore it. I don't know where I am or how much time passes as I lie here, feeling like I'm floating in a pool of water.

Hues of indigo bleed into the sky, and stars dust the heavens like glitter. I don't know what's happening, and my only conclusion is that I'm not where I'm supposed to be. Someone, somewhere, must be looking for me. I try to reach for any memory of *anything*, but all I get are images of people who look vaguely familiar.

I finally give up trying to make sense of what's going on, finding no answers in the vast sky nor the cool tingling that laps at my clothes and face. I wait until the pain in my gut recedes to a steady throb before I get up. Once I feel like I can do it without blacking out, I roll onto my knees and struggle to my feet. My limbs feel like weighted lead, and my head spins. I stand for about five seconds before collapsing on my face, submerged in milky white water.

*Pathetic, Travis,* I tell myself. At least I can recall my name. *You can't even stand.*

I push past the pain and exhaustion and get up for good. Staggering, I manage to keep my balance. I frown at my feet, ankle-deep in pale white water that seems to go on for miles when I look back up. Above me, the purple star-filled sky glistens and pulses. My clothes are dry despite the fact that I've lain in water for what might have been hours, and my coat flaps around in the windless air.

I wrack my mind for any past memories of this place, but it's beyond anything I've ever seen. The stars form pictures of people, places, words, and things, and somehow I know the pictures are of the past, present, and future. I'm seeing time as it is, yet it's not all there. Even with this knowledge, I can't come up with any idea of where I am, or if I'm dead or just dreaming. I shake my head and rub my eyes, trying to clear my mind. I have to get out of here, and standing around trying to figure out things I can't possibly understand won't help me.

Exhaling, I ignore the pain. I focus on my feet and take an unsteady step toward the expanse of vast nothingness before me. A soft ringing in my ears turns into a harsh whistle. The water ripples, and the swirling indigo sky explodes.

# Chapter I

## —Jack—

## Headaches

I'm jolted awake by another strange dream that leaves behind pain. I sit up in my bunk and rub my temples. Ever since I learned how to control where I go when I sleep, I've been searching. Sometimes I visit other friends, like Thomas Nowak, Cali Smith, Nora Moreau, or my little brother, Nico. Other times, I try to find our missing friend, Travis Knight. I have to believe he is alive; if not for the ever-growing guilt and remorse gnawing at me, for the sake of the world. He's the only other person holding the same dangerous weapon as me, after all.

Every night I try to find him, I wake up in head-splitting pain. I don't want to think about what this means—if this is what happens when I search for someone who no longer exists.

My dreams are the only proof of an existing connection, but I can never find him in them. Vivid and often short, I find myself standing in a field covered in white, with towering rocks casting shadows on both sides. Sometimes I dream of paved streets and steel buildings. It's frigid there, and I always wake up shivering.

Besides the dreams, I'm back in my old routine, though I'm not scavenging as much as before. There isn't a lot to do around camp except for packing. Ever since the battle between an Evil team and a large group of neutral people, the Indifferents, our camp has been preparing to either move into the Indifferents' building or find a more suitable location to settle down in.

The Indifferents have also been sending in monthly shipments. Bringing over people and supplies to pitch in as well as regulate the camp and make sure we're doing alright.

I hoist myself out of my bunk and put on work clothes—a plain white shirt with a gray-green coat, pants, and my leather boots. I brush my teeth and attempt to comb my tangled brown hair. The stone, a piece of technology that enhances my ability, MindSpeak, sits on my pillow. I grab it, and it melts into a bracelet fit specifically for my wrist. The stone allows me to access other people's minds, along with my usual ability to broadcast my thoughts without physically speaking, and to go into other people's dreams.

Some of the others are still sleeping; the work schedule isn't as tight as it used to be, so the Captain doesn't call attendance in the mornings anymore. The Long Room is mostly vacant.

"Jack!" a voice calls.

I turn around to see Thomas standing in the doorway. "Hey. What's up?"

He looks over his shoulder, nervously fiddling with a piece of string. "It's Nora."

"What happened?" I ask, worried, because Nora often strays from camp for hours before coming back.

"She's gone," Thomas answers softly.

"She'll come back."

"No, I mean, she left a note and everything."

I blink. I know Nora always talked about going on an adventure with the Indifferents or joining a new Good team, but I never expected her to just leave without telling us first.

Thomas holds up a wrinkled piece of notebook paper to my face, then turns it around and reads, *"Jack, Thomas, Cali, Kappa, thank you for everything. I'm sorry to say, but I can't stay here and act like things are normal. The Indifferents are amazing, but they spend too much time watching instead of doing. There is a war going on, after all, and at the end of the day, I'm a Good through and through. This is my ultimate choice, and I want to try my best to make a change. I hope to see you all again. Much love, Nora."*

"She can't be serious," I mutter.

Thomas shakes his head. "Her stuff is gone. It's like she was never here. No one saw her leave, either. The Captain has put our side of the Quarter on lockdown for now."

I huff, crossing my arms. We need Nora. Besides, the letter is too vague and not the kind of closure I can accept. And why a lockdown? I know it's dangerous, but I'm not scared anymore.

"We've ventured out of camp without permission once," I say. "We'd be able to do it again."

"Jack, that was once before, and because of an invasion no less. We didn't have a choice. If we go out again and get captured or worse, we could be risking everything the Indifferents have built. Everything we went through to keep the stone safe," Thomas reasons.

I try to come up with a counterargument, but my mind draws a blank. He's right, but that doesn't make the situation itself right. Besides, we were just getting settled back at camp. Yet something within me almost agrees with her—that restless part of me that wants to make a bigger difference than I have been here, which isn't much of a difference at all. Why did Nora have to go? And why didn't she take me with her?

"Look, I'm sure she'll end up coming back one way or another, right?" Thomas says.

I nod slowly, but I don't believe it. Nora has nothing to lose now. She's cut herself off from us, the only ones holding her back. What she said makes sense, too.

*The Indifferents are amazing, but they spend too much time watching instead of doing.*

"No, she's gone," I say, shaking my head. "We can't relax now, especially since both Nora and Travis are out. I know Travis is alive, and he has a part of the stone, too. But Nora's alone. I don't doubt her, but we—we could, I dunno, make sure she's alright. What if we went after—"

"You're kidding." Thomas crosses his arms. "No way."

I remember Nora's fierce determination, her steady and constant positivity and strength. The way she supported and encouraged everyone in the group, no matter how long she'd known them. Nora always jumped to help people, and I can't let her down when it's my turn.

Huffing, I cross my arms too. "It was just an idea."

Brief irritation flashes in Thomas's normally gentle brown eyes. "Jack, this is insane. Come on. You're not seriously going to leave now too? I told you this because I didn't want you to be confused and run out trying to find her, but it turns out you're still going to do that."

"Things change all the time," I hiss. "If you're not willing to move forward, then the rest of the world will leave you behind. Besides, I never said I was going anywhere."

"We *are* moving forward!" he says, his usually level tone rising. "That's why we're packing and moving with the Indifferents. It's Nora who took it too far. She must have a death wish or something."

I flinch, clenching my teeth. "Nora's going to make a change. Isn't it a good idea that we follow her?"

"No, Jack, it's too dangerous."

"Or maybe you're just too *scared.*"

Thomas's annoyed expression melts into a mask of hurt. Spiking guilt and realization replace my earlier indignance. I didn't think before speaking. Thomas and I have never gotten into an argument before. Not once. But judging by his wounded look, I crossed a line.

I avert my gaze, feeling ashamed. He stares at me for a second before shouldering past and grabbing some of his things.

"Thomas, I'm sorry—"

"It's fine." His back is turned to me, and his voice is tight.

He exhales, finds what he needs, and leaves without another word.

I stand in the doorway, unsure of what to think. I'm so stupid. I didn't consider Thomas's feelings and personal life in all of this. Come to think of it, have I ever thought about what Thomas and Cali may be going through? Leaving everything familiar and embarking on a journey into a land unknown? Of course they'd be scared; we all were. And yet they still went on the journey with me. I never really took into account how brave they are.

I had no right to call Thomas a coward.

A familiar panic creeps back into my mind. How many people's lives have I endangered just in the span of a few months? How many times have I taken advantage of my friends' loyalty?

I shake my head, trying to clear my mind. I haven't decided to leave. Not yet. I still need to consult with everyone else. I massage my temples again, my headache coming back. Inhaling deeply, I walk out the door.

# Chapter II

## —Travis—

## **Wake Up**

I jolt forward, a sudden sense of panic and urgency spiking through my body. My rapidly beating heart matches my quick and shallow breaths, and my fingers close around emptiness.

The world is a freezing, empty void. I can't see, though there's a faint, familiar smell, like the gritty scent of charcoal. I scrabble at the ground beneath me, trying to get a feel for where I am. My blunt nails hit a rough stone floor, cold, just like everything else. Adrenaline courses through my veins as I blink, testing my vision, but it's still empty. I try to calm down and listen, but all I can hear is the thumping of my heart and the ringing in my ears.

Light flickers, and suddenly my vision comes tumbling back. Cool relief washes through me, and my heart rate drops a bit as I start to calm down. I'm in some sort of pocket in a cliffside, judging from the cave opening that extends back into a wide tunnel. A dim fire crackles in front of me, casting my shadow against the jagged and rough walls. The wind whistles outside, along with angrily fluttering white powder that blows past the wide entrance.

Snowstorm. Blizzard.

The two words pop into my mind at the sight of ice and snow. I shiver, edging myself closer to the dying fire. A thin blanket is draped around my shoulders. I pick at my frozen clothing only to find itchy bandages covering my torso. I'm too numb to feel any of the pain, but by the look of the bloody bandages, the wound isn't very happy with me. I hold my hands out to the fire, my slender fingers arching over the flames in hopes of returning the color to their bluish tone. Ripped black fabric covers my knuckles, wound tightly enough around that it hurts.

I try not to dwell on the frustrating questions, focusing instead on surviving. But I can't help wondering how I got here or where the fire, blanket, and bandages came from. I want to know what's going on, but hypothermia is more pressing. Besides, I can't even answer the easiest things—exactly how much time has passed or what happened to me that landed me in the middle of nowhere in a snowstorm. It can't have been long. My wound is still fairly recent, judging from the blood. And yet, my memories of before the shift, before I got here, feel distant. The more I try to piece the fragments of my memory together, the more jumbled they become.

It isn't that I can't remember anything. My memory, as far as I know, seems intact up until my world switches to *this*. I can recall events, people, places. My name is Travis Knight. I turned sixteen on my last birthday, which was somewhere in the late winter season. I've known a girl named Nora Moreau since I was four. My mom died in a battle. My father disappeared on a mission. I made friends with three kids and a robot not too long ago.

No, I know my own history. But the whole process of remembering feels like I'm learning about a different person. It's like reading a book about someone else. Someone else whose tragic life would almost be comical if that someone else weren't me.

I snap out of my daze and get back to business—patting my clothes down and trying to find any weapons that the previous me would have conveniently left on my person before he decided to die. My recollection of that event has a couple of understandable gaps, though I distinctly remember the faces that crowded around me as I blinked in and out of consciousness before fully losing my grip. Rowan—of all people, I had to be taken out by him. Part of me is angry at myself for letting it happen. Though, thinking back on it, I don't regret taking a bullet meant for Nora.

I find a gun strapped to my belt, but it's empty. Great. I don't bother taking off my boots to check for knives hidden in the special sheaths sewn on the inside, as my feet are cold enough as it is.

My gaze drifts from the fire to the rest of the cave. I note the space in the back enveloped in shadows. The blizzard outside seems lighter. I force the headache that's waiting to erupt away from the forefront of my mind. If there's anything I know about myself, it's that I don't waste time dwelling on things that aren't useful in the moment. I'll freeze to death if the only thing I have is a poor fire and my thoughts to keep me going. That's unacceptable. Right now I need to find a way to help the fire, perhaps find some more wood or any substitutes, and then set out once the blizzard clears.

I roll into a kneeling position and push myself off the ground. Nausea hits me immediately, my body ringing the familiar warning bells that mean starvation and probably severe iron deficiency. I stumble into the wall, barely feeling the rocky surface digging into my shoulder. After a few ragged breaths, I'm able to steady myself and stand up straight with minimal cursing. As I shift, something falls out of the folds of my blanket and clatters to the floor. I struggle to bend and pick up the object, wondering how I didn't find it earlier. It's an indigo stone that glows faintly, casting a soft purple light on the walls and ceiling. It's about the size of an egg, twisted in a strange oblong shape. And it's warm, incredibly and soothingly warm.

Holding it up, I study it, examining every side. It flashes, startling me, but I don't drop it. It turns into a small dagger in my hand. A memory pops up of a friend. Jack. He's an annoying and endearing kid who helped me remember how to be human through his compassion. Sentiment aside, he had an aqua stone that could take on multiple forms. It was important. There was a battle fought over it, and then—

"Hello?"

My muddled senses switch to high alert. I back deeper into the cave, away from the light of the fire, carefully hiding my glowing weapon under my blanket. A figure stands at the mouth of the cave holding a bundle of sticks and branches.

"Hello?" a feminine voice calls again. "Are you there?"

I shuffle backward until I brush up against the end of the cave. I'm completely concealed by the darkness, watching the figure cautiously, my fingers tightening around the hilt of the blade. I breathe out of my mouth so I'm quieter. The only noises are the crackling fire and her uncertain footsteps farther into the cave.

The stranger tentatively walks to the fire, drops the firewood so it clatters against the stone, then starts walking toward me. I tense, prepared to attack.

She's five feet away, three feet away—

I body-slam her, my knife drawn as she stumbles back into the wall. She yelps, waving her arms in defense. I flip the dagger around so I'm holding the blade away from me, and I press my forearm against her throat, using my height and what strength I have left to pin her to the wall.

"You—you're awake," she squeaks.

She has short platinum hair that falls around her shoulders, fair skin, and pale green-gray eyes that glint with fear. Her warm winter coat is covered in snow.

"I'm very much awake," I agree, not letting up.

"Where—Where did you get that knife?" she croaks, her eyes wide in shock.

"Where am I?" I demand.

"J—Just an hour or so's walk from the city walls," she chokes out. "Can you let me go?"

City walls.

The thought of being near the city where I died quickly passes through my mind. That city may be chilly, but outside it is a hot desert. No, I conclude, we're nowhere near the preferred city.

"What city?" I ask. "Where are we on the world map? In the eastern or southern continents? What region is this?"

She makes a little sound in the back of her throat, and I realize she can't answer with me pressing down so hard. I back up enough to let her speak.

"The City of Kaltic. Wh—What do you mean, 'world map'?"

I exhale. "You know, a map of the entire world?"

I wrack my mind for memories of Kaltic, but nothing comes up. Named cities are usually important, but I have no knowledge of this one. And oddly enough, this girl has no idea what a world map is, which is concerning. Most people have a general idea of the rest of the world if they're not totally isolated or secluded from it.

The girl interrupts my train of thought. "No, I *don't* know. I'm not stupid; I know what a map is. But the entire world? What do you mean?" She sounds more indignant than scared now.

I blink slowly, taken aback. "The entire world, like, regions and groups of people and landmasses, on a map. Continents and cities and ports—all that stuff."

Her eyes light up, and under her breath I hear her mutter, "Of course."

I try a different question. "What am I doing here?"

"I—I found you in the snow just outside the city limits. I was just, uh, taking a walk, but I've never encountered outsiders before in all of my seventeen years, though I do know they exist," she rambles.

"Okay, okay. So do you have weapons on you?"

"W—Weapons? No, of course not."

"Are you sure?"

"Yes."

I stare at her for a couple of seconds, but her expression makes it clear she's not lying.

"What's your name?" I ask.

"Name?" she repeats. "Names are for the Important."

I sigh, trying not to think about that strange statement, assuming it's more of her weird not-know-what-a-world-map-is mentality. "How are you addressed? What do others call you?"

"O—Oh," she stammers. "My code is HG-8057."

I pause. Code?

"No, Like, my *name* is Travis. Surely you're called something other than letters and numbers?"

"Tra-vis." She sounds out my name slowly, grinning. "Amazing."

"Yes." I grit my teeth, getting irritated.

"I have no name," she murmurs, her smile slipping. "It's HG-8057. It always has been. It always will be."

"I'm not calling you that. It's hardly appropriate, and it's too much of a mouthful."

I stagger away from her. Determining she's no threat, I lower my weapon and face the cave opening, hugging the blanket tighter around my shoulders.

"We need to call you *something*," I mutter, a little deliriously.

She steps away from the wall carefully, making her way to the fire. "Like what?"

"I'll just call you HG," I sigh. "That's easier to remember at least."

"Alright." She grins. "It's a start."

I allow myself a little smile. I don't know HG, but she saved me, and since I don't know where I am, it's good to have an ally who knows the area. Better to get along with her for those reasons.

"Travis," she says, warming up to my name.

"Yeah?"

"How are you feeling?"

I turn my gaze away from the entrance. It's not a question I get often with that much sincerity. For a good portion of my life, that question was specifically withheld from Evils and only used on sick people.

"A bit dizzy. 'M fine," I respond, my words starting to slur together.

"Are you hungry?" She seems concerned, even though the first thing I did was pull a knife on her.

"A little," I confess, choosing survival over pride. The nausea from before hasn't completely subsided.

"I—I have some food. You should eat, you don't look too well."

"Right, thanks."

She scrambles to take the pack off her shoulder and rifle through it, producing a packet of dried jerky.

I steady myself against the wall again, sliding down until my knees hit the ground. I'm more exhausted than I initially realized. I shiver. The only feeling in my body is the tiny chill that runs up and down my neck and arms.

HG hurries over to me, her knee-length boots padding softly on the cave floor. She rests her hand on my forehead as if I have a fever.

I flinch away from her, not fond of the intimate touch. She sees my discomfort and apologizes quickly, then takes off her giant coat and hands it to me.

"Here," she mutters. "You're quite cold."

She's only wearing a simple long-sleeved shirt, but I can't protest. My body is numb, and the persistent bluish tinge in my fingertips doesn't seem like a good sign. At this point, staying alive is more important than being polite, not that the latter sits high on my list. I nod and take the coat, wrapping it around myself and burying my head in the fluffy hood. It smells like soap and smoke, and reminds me of home, wherever that went.

HG hands me the jerky. "If you finish it and are still hungry, I have more provisions in the jacket pocket."

"Thanks," I murmur.

I open the packet she gave me with trembling fingers and scarf it all down, eating quickly out of habit. I don't stop to savor the food, I just eat.

HG watches me in quiet fascination, as if she's never seen a hungry person eat before. Or perhaps she's never seen a person like me before. Either way, her staring is disconcerting, and ally or not, I don't tolerate it. I shoot her a sharp glance, hoping my expression tells her to knock it off.

She quickly turns her attention to the fire, setting pieces of kindling on the embers. I frown when she pushes one of the larger, more noticeably frozen and wet, branches in.

"You're not really good at making fires," I comment. "'S more like a pile of soggy twigs with a matchstick in the middle."

She looks up at me, startled. "W—Well, I—"

"'S okay." I quickly amend my muddled brain-to-mouth note. "Try using the drier pieces o' wood."

She looks disappointedly at her tiny fire and sighs. "This won't work."

"Nah, but I can help you," I say, recalling the special matches my previous Evil team gave me, and wondering if I had some tucked away in my boot, the only place I hadn't checked.

"No, Travis, I mean …" She pauses, glaring at the fire. "This whole thing. It's a lost cause."

I cock an eyebrow. "Mm?"

"All I want is to just be away from that place. It's infuriating, being cooped up in the city." She sniffles, and it takes me a second to realize she's close to tears. "I've been trying to flee Kaltic for *years* now, determined there's something else out there, but I always end up returning. There is no escape from Kaltic. It is all there is left. There is nothing *but* Kaltic. We need to go back at some point."

I stare at her, soaking in her words. Kaltic is a city, but she can't seem to leave it permanently for some reason. Something tells me it may be more than just the snow and weather. A disconcerting feeling settles in the pit of my stomach at that. If it's so bad that she's been trying to leave all this time, why are we going back?

"You're wrong," I tell her. "There's always somethin' out there. Wherever we are, we'll find it."

Her pale, watery eyes regard me pensively. "We are surrounded by mountains. Even outside the city walls, we are trapped." Her brows furrow in frustration. "But at least when I'm out here, I have some semblance of freedom."

"Tha''s t—tough," I stutter, my teeth chattering. I clench my jaw. "R—Regardless, there has to be a way out o' here. Can't sit 'ere forever."

"The storm is letting up just a bit," she whispers, drying her eyes with her sleeve. "I'm afraid we should be heading back to Kaltic. I've been gone too long, and you need help."

I study her warily. "'S it warm there?"

"Inside the buildings, yes."

With a nod, I decide that Kaltic is my best bet. I rationalize that if HG can just take a walk outside the city, it shouldn't be too hard for me to leave, despite her ominous warnings.

She turns to look at me. "Oh, that doesn't look good at all."

I don't appreciate the expression of pity mixed with concern. Using the wall for support, I get up shakily and walk to the entrance of the cave where the storm has died down, leaving behind a thick blanket of snow.

"'M fine," I repeat, taking a step outside. "Le''s … go."

And with that bit of eloquence, I collapse into the white snow as the exhaustion and cold finally sink their claws into my mind. The white turns to purple, and I start falling, falling through time, falling through a cloud of indigo.

# Chapter III

## —Jack—

## Slice

The Captain took me off Scavenger duty for the day. The denial was so abrupt, I thought Thomas had told him of our earlier argument. But surely Thomas, of all people, wouldn't rat me out. Especially since I hadn't said I was going anywhere.

For the most part, it's been quiet around the camp. After the battle, Thala and Cole spoke with me about the stone, but I haven't seen either of them recently. Thala's the leader of the Indifferents, so it'd make sense she's busy. It's been peaceful, which is a relief, if only I wasn't still a huge risk and liability to the safety of my own camp.

I asked Cole, back in our meeting, why he didn't just take the stone and hide it away again. He's the one who created it, and the one who placed it in this city, after all. Concealing it seemed less risky and would probably spare us from the potential war the stone could spark. After all, both the Goods and Evils knew about it. It was simply too dangerous.

Cole frowned, crossed his arms and said, "I hid it once, and you found it. And then they found you. They have ways of tracking it. As long as it is with you, I know it will be in safe, reliable hands."

"Now the battle's over," I muttered, looking at the floor, "why still entrust it to me? Why not an adult?"

"You have the most experience with it," he told me. "You are the best qualified to keep it. You did say you were up to the task, yes?"

I nodded grimly.

"Do not worry, Jack," he assured me. "You're not alone in this."

At camp, they don't supervise me like I thought they would after the battle. I keep up my usual job, except on the days I'm assigned to something else for whatever reason the Captain has.

Like now.

He has me working in the kitchen with Cali, which gives me the opportunity to discuss Nora's situation with her. She doesn't seem surprised in the slightest.

I angrily chop a bell pepper, one of the imports from the main Indifferents building. Supposedly, they come from the top floor, where they have a huge indoor garden. The dome at the top is made of glass and lets the sunlight in, and that's how they're able to get different types of produce in the middle of a desert.

That's one of the perks about joining the Indifferents—the new, fresh food. And we don't even have to trade for it.

"I still don't get why I got demoted," I complain to Cali after a moment of quiet accompanied by the knife connecting with the chopping board.

"Kitchen duty isn't a demotion," she says. "He probably just called for the lockdown as a precaution. So no one else ends up disappearing, y' know?"

"Disappearing?" a voice echoes from the entrance to the kitchen.

I turn to see my little brother, Nico, in the doorway. He's grown an inch, and I don't doubt he'll pass me soon.

His rust-colored hair has also grown, so he'll need a haircut in a few days as well.

"Hey, Nico," I say.

"What were you guys talking about?" he asks, his emerald eyes wide.

"Whatcha doing here, Nico?" I dodge, turning my attention back to my knife and the bell peppers.

"I'm on break," he explains, brushing off my answer.

"Nice," I say. "Where's Mom and Dad?"

"Working," he mutters, his eyes downcast. "They're always working."

I exhale. "Well, dinner's in fifteen minutes, so you should be able to see them soon."

"I wanna hang out with you guys, though," he says.

I give a strained smile. "Sure, yeah."

Nico hops into the kitchen, watching us work. I glance at him and he grins, rocking on his heels.

"You want help?" he asks, bouncing up to me.

I wave him off with my free hand. "Nah, we're good. Thank you, though."

"Mhm." He peers over my shoulder. "Can I try that?"

"By itself?"

"Yeah!" His eyes are wide, eager.

I pick one of the chopped pieces and hand it to him, lowering my voice. "Alright, just don't tell anyone."

He pops it into his mouth. "Hmm … it's alright."

Nico buzzes away to explore the kitchen. Cali hums to herself, now stacking trays. With nothing to keep my mind occupied other than the task at hand, it wanders back to the morning. Is Thomas still mad? The prickle of doubt and guilt poke at me, reminding me of all the ways I could have gone about speaking to him.

"Watch your finger, Jack," Cali warns.

I stop my knife just in time. It hovers over my left hand.

"Thanks, Cali," I say.

"No problem." She chuckles. "Would hate to see you lose a finger."

I grin. "Right."

We finish with our tasks in time to get ready for dinner. My stomach churns at the thought of seeing Thomas again, especially after our recent episode. I hope he's okay by now. I know I'm sure not. I'm conflicted over everything. My friends mean a lot to me. I already lost Nora, and I didn't even do anything. Knowing I could easily lose Thomas as well, because of my own actions, makes me apprehensive.

The tension is like a blade above my hand. One false move and I lose a digit. Only, when it comes to my friends, I have more to lose than just a finger.

# Chapter IV

## —Travis—

## **Twice Rise**

The gray ceiling above me stares back dully. It's so quiet, I can hear the faint tick of the wall clock's needle as it counts the seconds. A faint, bitter smell hangs in the air, reminding me of early mornings, but my mind is too addled to place it.

I don't know how I got here, though I remember someone lifting me and my feet dragging in the cold slush of the snow. I recall reaching a sort of gate, and people surrounding me. There were shouts, and then rough hands grabbing me.

So here I am.

It's been a few hours, I think. I've been drifting in an out of consciousness and haven't checked the clock.

Groaning, I sit up and stretch my cramped muscles. My surroundings are dull, yet neat and clean. The white walls blend in with the gray floor and gray ceiling. I'm sitting on a hard cot in the corner of a small room, a cell, perhaps. The brick walls make the room seem purposed for confinement. There are no windows, just a door opposite my cot.

I'm disconcerted to realize I'm wearing new clothes—a white long-sleeved shirt and gray pants. The stone is still on my wrist, confusing me for a second, though I remember Jack carried his stone the same way. The black cloth around my hands is gone, revealing odd burn marks on my knuckles. My boots, thankfully, are lined up next to my cot, but after a quick search, I find nothing.

The rest of the small room is empty.

I lean over the edge of the cot, tilting onto my feet. I don't have socks on, and the cold of the floor soaks into my bare skin. Kneeling down, I slip on the boots, figuring I'd rather get blisters from not having socks than frostbite from not having shoes.

I'm a little lightheaded, but overall, nothing hurts too bad—a slight throb in my abdomen and in my temples. The lack of pain makes me wonder if I'm on some sort of medication, or if my wounds were magically healed, though I doubt the second thought. The bandages are newly changed. I notice blood starting to dot on them, so I leave them alone.

The door has no windows or even a handle, just a crack in the wall indicating hinges and a padlock where a handle should go. But with my capabilities, who needs handles?

Pressing myself into the door, I feel the familiar tingle I get when I casually fade through solid objects. I don't hang onto my senses with this shift. I can keep my eyesight or hearing if I concentrate, but doing so is more exhausting. My body turns numb, then I'm standing in the hallway outside my cell. My senses start coming back in a rush; first touch, then hearing, then sight. I blink the dark spots away and rub my arms and hands in an attempt to warm myself up. The hallway is long and brightly lit, and there are no guards outside like I had expected. I assume I'm in Kaltic, the city HG spoke of before I passed out in the cave.

*This is easy*, I think as I roll my shoulders.

I survey the hallway for any other threats. It sure is cold, but I can adapt. I need to find HG or someone I can use to help me. If all else fails, I'm sure I can storm the place myself and get answers. And then I can get out of here and find my friends.

Double doors at the end of the hallway have handles, but I find they're locked too. I pass through them like I did before but stumble when I come out on the other side, my senses lagging more.

"I told you to stop!" a female voice commands, her words growing louder as my hearing returns.

My first thought is, *Thala?* as my mind associates the first time I ran into the Indifferents back in the desert, when Thala and her army surrounded us. Then my instincts push me to my usual tactic of attacking first and asking questions after. I lunge blindly toward the voice. My sight returns when I already have the target pinned down, my stone a thin indigo knife tilted sideways with the edge of the blade underneath her chin.

Surrounding us are people all wearing the same uniform. Some are sitting at tables, all are frozen, staring at me in shock. I'm kneeling over a tough-looking woman. Her black hair is cut short and raggedy, as if she trimmed it with a pair of shears, and she's built like a fighter—stocky and muscular. She stares back at me, stunned, as if she hadn't expected a person half her age to overpower her so suddenly.

I can't leverage surprise any longer. She throws her weight and flips us around, and I narrowly dodge a fist. Using all my strength to knee her in the gut, I scoot out from under her. There's no ringing of shots fired, and no one else in the circle has made much of a move, so I'm not too concerned just yet.

My opponent backs up onto her feet, squaring her shoulders. She's slowly reaching for a device on her belt that looks suspiciously like a transceiver.

"Stop," I growl, twirling the dagger in my hand.

"Where did you get that?" she asks, a hint of fear in her otherwise balanced voice.

I smile. "How about you answer my question. Where am I?"

"I am not obligated to tell you anything." Her voice doesn't waver, impressively, but I can see the panic in her eyes.

"Ma'am!" shouts a boy as he stands. He's at a table with five soldiers. He can't be much older than me. "What are your orders?"

"Fetch the Axe, AR-6180," she commands. "We have a level-two threat."

He nods, turning on his heel toward the door opposite the one I faded through. I catch his pale blue gaze and, in a flash, my knife shifts into a gun. I swivel the barrel of my firearm and train it on him, an unspoken message saying, *Don't move.*

He halts, eyeing me warily. I can't pick out fear in his steady expression, only uncertainty.

"Nobody moves. Nobody contacts *anyone*," I say, mustering the Evil voice I used when I was still on the team. "Or he earns an early mortality. After him, your leader is next."

The woman's jaw is set, and she glares at me as she speaks. "Do as he says."

"Put your hands where I can see them, and don't try anything," I add, my gaze flicking around the circle. "If anyone so much as breathes wrong, our friend AR gets it."

"Let us resolve this peacefully," the woman hisses. "There does not have to be bloodshed."

"Well, of course." I let my expression slide into a condescending smirk. "Do as I say, and no one gets hurt. Simple as that."

"I'm afraid we cannot allow that. You are being detained until further notice. That is the process with all outsiders."

I roll my shoulders. "I'm sure this 'process' is very, very different. Have you ever reached a stalemate with any of your other outsiders?"

I take their silence as a no.

"Right, so," I start, clearing my throat. "I'm not staying here."

The woman opens her mouth to protest.

"No, shut up," I tell her, holding out my free palm. "It's not up for discussion. And while I'd love to stay and chat with you all, I have some things to do."

I survey the faces of the soldiers, trying to piece together my next steps. I need supplies, first of all, but if I tell them outright, they'll have the upper hand, since they'll just follow me. Warm clothes and food—I should be able to get those judging from the way these people are dressed. They don't look like they're starving, either. As for the map, I'll have to find the right sources. By HG's reaction, there might not be one easily available.

"Alright," I say after an uncomfortable pause, pointing my chin at AR, who's still standing idly by the door. "You're coming with me."

"Why?" he asks, and I almost can't believe the audacity. Mostly because it reminds me of myself.

"Because I said so. Got a problem?"

He stares at me blankly before shrugging casually, much to the dismay of his fellow soldiers.

"AR-6180, don't—" the woman starts.

"Hey," I warn, pitching my voice down in a creepily accurate impersonation of one of the leaders from my Evil team.

She ignores me, whipping around to AR, her brows furrowed. "Don't go, AR-6180."

He bows his head. "For Kaltic."

"*That's an order*," she adds, and finally I can hear the frustrated desperation in her voice.

"I don't think you get it," I say, stepping forward. My body shimmers as I start to fade again, this time focusing on keeping my vision while my other senses go dull.

Her eyes narrow, and she says something. Perhaps she's prompting me to continue.

I point my gun at AR. "He doesn't have a choice."

I start walking toward AR and the door. Right as I near her, she swings her fist at me, aimed for the side of my head. Her punch would be fast enough to knock me out, and the accuracy is terrifyingly perfect. I don't blink when her fist connects with where my jaw would be and passes through. She stumbles forward. I glance back as her knees hit the floor, and she recoils, staring at her fingers. I keep walking, ignoring the fuzzy tingling in my skull from where her hand shimmered through.

"Don't try anything," I repeat over my shoulder as I point AR forward.

He nods at the woman, then at me, and opens the door. I slip out behind him, allowing myself to revert. He doesn't have a weapon—none of them do for some odd reason—and I'm still armed, so if he does decide to attack, I have a couple of advantages. My nullified senses rush back, along with a slight throbbing in my temples.

A spike of adrenaline thrills through me as I try to logically assess and reassess the new situation I've put myself in. I feel eerily calm despite the thrumming in my head, though I've never really been one to panic while on the move. Of course, I don't trust AR, and part of me wonders what his angle is. Whether it's the soldiers' training or just AR's personality, he didn't seem all too concerned with being threatened, and lack of fear is questionable in hostages. I watch the back of his head, and something unsettling stirs in my gut. Dread, or hunger, or a bit of both.

Then again, I don't have a better option for now.

Following AR, I slip out into the winter sun.

# Chapter V

## —Jack—

## Names

Thomas sits with us as usual, though he's quiet. Cali sits next to me, and Kappa sits across from us, watching us eat. It's a little unsettling, but I know that's just how she is. The Dining Hall is packed with people sitting at large rectangular tables that are lined up from wall to wall. The chatter is loud but not annoyingly so. With the warm lantern lights and casual atmosphere, it feels like home. But even in the familiar air of the Hall, a level of discomfort hangs over our table until Nico deftly quashes it with his talkative nature.

"Did you know Mom and Dad are leading a new mission now? It was a last-minute decision, but they stepped in for someone who got sick. They'll have to leave again," he exclaims.

"Well, that's no fun," I say between bites, not in the mood for chitchat.

"I hope they get to come back quickly. Do you think they'll want to move to the Indifferents' building, stay here, or join the new colony? I want to see the main building. You said it's really big, right? It's in a desert, right? Are cactuses real? Is it cactuses or cacti? Nora told me words sometimes get changed when there's many of the word. Where is Nora, anyway?"

"*Nicholas.*" I grit my teeth, the headache from earlier threatening to come back.

"I want to join the main building, Nico," Cali butts in. "There are no cactuses, and I'm not too sure if it's cacti. Nora's pretty smart, huh? She went off exploring."

I pass Cali a look of gratitude for taking Nico off my hands, though I always feel guilty when my friends are nicer to him than I am. Mom always said I'm too serious, though that can't be true. I play around just as much as the next guy. Thomas is a lot more serious than me.

"Thomas, eat your food," Kappa chides in her singsong voice.

I notice he's been swirling his vegetables around, as if lost in thought.

He looks up. "Oh, yeah. Sheesh, Kappa, I already have one mom."

She tilts her head and stares at him quizzically. "You all speak of 'mom.' What is mom?"

"Mom is just a more casual word for 'mother,'" a new voice answers from behind us.

I whip around to see the Captain with his own tray of sustenance, towering over us with that unfair height of his.

"May I dine with you?" the Captain asks, though it's not really a question.

He has this way of saying things like he's barking an order. I don't think he can ask questions.

"Yeah, of course," Nico pipes up, patting the empty seat beside him.

The Captain walks around the table and sets his tray down carefully next to Nico. I've never had dinner with the Captain. I'm more comfortable with his presence since the battle. We all have been, my brother especially. Nico told me the Captain looked out for everyone, staying a strong figure in the face of the Evils, even when the other leaders were distressed and hopeless.

"How have you been, Nicholas?" the Captain asks.

"Good. How about you, Alistair?" Nico responds.

Hold up. *Alistair?*

Even Thomas turns to look at them, confused. Cali smirks at us knowingly. I blink, trying to process what I just heard.

"Eat your food, Thomas," Kappa repeats.

I stare at the Captain. "Alistair?"

"Yes?" he says, returning my gaze.

"Your name is *Alistair*?"

He raises an eyebrow. "Did you think my name was 'The Captain?'"

"Well, yes— I mean no, of course not! I knew you had a name, I just didn't— I never thought—" I stumble over my words, unsure of myself.

His dark eyes twinkle, amused. "I suppose it is a common misconception. Actually, my rank isn't captain. When I was your age, my friends gave me that nickname because I apparently bossed everyone around. It stuck and has been passed down. No one questions it anymore, or bothers asking. They just hear others call me Captain and accept it."

"Oh." I try to process his words. "How old are you now? You say 'when I was your age' like it was a long time ago."

"I'm twenty-four," he replies, chuckling. "Why? Do I look old?"

My face flushes. "No, you just seem older than … I don't know. Never mind."

Cali laughs. "You seriously haven't known his real name until now?"

"No," I say quietly, and Thomas looks down, embarrassed.

"Wait, Nico," I say. "When did you find out?"

He swallows a mouthful of warm bread, courtesy of the Indifferents. "Just last month."

"Oh."

"We're good friends."

"Oh."

I finish off my plate just as quietly as Thomas, who finally starts eating after Kappa's third or fourth round of insisting. She talks to us too, but most of her concerns are pointed at Thomas. He's the first person she turns to when given a situation she needs a decision on.

Cali stretches, getting up with her clean tray. "Well, I'm heading to bed. G'night, guys."

"'Night," I say.

Thomas responds with a halfhearted, "Goodnight," and Nico gives her a hug before she leaves.

"Barret," the Captain—or Alistair, whatever—addresses me.

"Yes, sir?"

"Can I trust you on a scavenging job tomorrow?" he asks. This time it sounds like a question.

"Yes, sir."

"You won't run off looking for Nora?"

"H—Huh? Run off?" I feign ignorance. "No, of course not."

His eyes narrow as if he's trying to discern a lie. Then his shoulders drop, reminding me of the weary state I found him in when I spoke to him in a dream before the battle.

"Very well," he says.

"Thank you, sir," I reply.

"Curfew's in fifteen minutes."

"Yes, sir."

I wait for Thomas and Nico to finish eating before I get up. We allow Nico to lead us back to the Long Room.

It's in a new location, ever since the siege and battle. Some of the other boys are already there, sleeping or milling about.

I brush my teeth, take off my work clothes and boots, and tuck Nico in. All the routine of getting ready for bed feels so normal, and yet, nothing has been the same for me since the battle. It doesn't seem right to go back to how things were before; it's as if everyone just forgot.

Maybe Thomas is right, but I want to at least check if Nora's safe. Luckily for me, I have just the ability to do that.

I climb up into my bunk, feeling nervous and jittery as well as calm. Nervous and jittery because of all the thoughts bouncing around my mind. Calm because I know no one can hear those thoughts. Not anymore.

The Captain walks in and calls lights-out in his commanding tone. The lights flick off, drenching the room in familiar darkness. I close my eyes, knowing where I want to go.

I need to speak to Nora.

# Chapter VI

## —Travis—

## Facts

I follow AR around the block, pretending to be unbothered by the stinging cold. The atmosphere is bright and crisp, the winter sun barely masked by the white clouds that punctuate the pale blue sky. Tiny flakes of snow dance around us, melting on our skin and in our hair. It reminds me of a reverse flamestorm.

"Okay, wait," I say, raising my gun so it's level with his shoulder blades.

He turns around slowly, his gaze dipping down to my weapon before flicking back to my face.

"It's stupidly cold out here," I continue, ignoring how he rolls his eyes. "You have places where you store resources—clothing and food, right?"

"Of course," AR answers.

I glance around, then focus back on him. "Take me there."

He sighs a foggy cloud that dissipates into the frosty air, then turns back around, his pace picking back up.

AR isn't nervous, and he doesn't look back as I trail behind him. He strolls through the empty streets, taking turns around snow-covered brick buildings and passing lampposts with leisure. I observe the concrete streets for any signs of life, but they're devoid of people. Smoke ascends into the sky from the roofs, perhaps chimneys connected to furnaces or fireplaces to keep the insides warm. The four-story buildings form imposing shapes that guard this city's inhabitants. Though, the lack of people only makes Kaltic seem more threatening.

"Where are you from?" AR starts as we take a right turn. He's still facing forward.

"I didn't ask for an interrogation."

"Alright." He stops, his boots scraping against the pavement.

I halt beside him. "Keep going, it's freezing out here."

His piercing blue eyes narrow. "I'm sure you're aware that you have no idea where you are, and that I'm the only one you can trust to get you to those resources you need. It wouldn't hurt to answer the harmless questions of the *only* person willing to help you."

Setting my jaw, I raise an eyebrow at him. "Have you forgotten that we're not allies? I'm holding you at gunpoint. I'm sure your life is more important to you than my answers."

He's unimpressed at best, but he sighs and nods. "Fine. Come on."

AR picks up his pace again, leaving me to scamper after him to match his stride. The soles of my feet have gone numb, but there's a prickly sensation spiking through them with each step. I'm grateful that I still have my boots—it would be much worse without them.

I watch AR move fluidly through the streets, unbothered by the temperature. He seems bored almost, though I can't imagine how he can be so indifferent to the threat I pose. A nagging thought in the back of my mind tells me I should befriend him, so he becomes less of an unknown factor and more of an asset.

"I—" I pause, making sure he can hear me. "I don't know where I'm from. I moved around a lot growing up. My name is Travis."

He glances back at me. "You have a name?"

"Yeah, I know, names are for the Important, whatever that means," I say, sighing. "Well, out there, names are how we identify each other. Your parents or whoever raises you gives you a name, typically at birth."

He hums thoughtfully. "You shortened my code to 'AR' earlier."

"Yeah, it's easier to remember."

"I have a badge on my uniform with my code."

"It's also easier to pronounce. Are we almost there?"

"Five more minutes at this pace."

I exhale a puff of white into the frigid air and rub my face. "What's your rank, AR?"

"Corporal."

"You look pretty young," I remark, though it's not too surprising. I was promoted to a high-ranking leadership role in my old Evil team a few years ago.

He shrugs, facing forward. "Do you have cities like ours in the outside world? With militias as well?"

Kicking a clump of snow on the ground, I answer, "No, the cities aren't organized like yours. I assume you have some form of government, but out there, it's pretty much a free-for-all. Though, most of the world is on a side, so there is some organization in that sense."

"On a side?" he repeats. "What do you mean?"

"There are two sides—the Good and the Evil. Or that's their generalized titles, anyway. Each side has their own territory, and they both have a higher command. Within each side are many smaller teams, with about fifty to a hundred people, depending on how many families they host. We've— Uh … the two sides have been at war all over the world for years."

"What side are you on?" AR asks, picking up a more conversational tone.

"I'm … I'm not on a side. There are neutral people who either live in cities in unclaimed areas or travel around together. Out there are ports and big cities still running where a lot of people live. There is a sort of trading system, but a lot of it's industrialized depending on what city you're in and what side you're on."

"Interesting," he murmurs. "Tell me about how you're able to turn into a ghost."

I frown, not liking how AR managed to turn this into an interview. But I need him on my side, so I go along with it anyway.

"That's my ability. It allows me to pass through solid objects."

He clicks his tongue. "So that's how you escaped your cell. I've heard of the touched possessing strange powers, but seeing it in action makes it much more impressive."

"The 'touched,'" I parrot, my eyebrows furrowing. "You mean foreigners to your land … or people affected by radiation?"

"Yes," AR replies.

"Yes, as in which one?"

"Both. Every outsider we've gotten has been one of the touched. They are marked by odd capabilities, and our machines detect them as impure. Like you."

"So you do mean people born into radiation," I decide. "Okay."

"What's that? Radiation, I mean," he asks.

I rub my temples, reminding myself that he knows virtually nothing about the rest of the world. "Remember how I mentioned global wars? Well, those wars sparked new weapons. Those weapons gave off a deadly radiation that both killed and turned children born afterward into supernatural humans."

We round a corner for what seems like the hundredth time.

"So, if it killed people, how did the newborns survive?" AR asks.

"I'm … I'm not sure." I frown.

Normally I'd have some sort of answer. I've learned a lot of things. And yet, I've never really thought of it that way, never bothered asking.

AR stops in front of a white brick building. "We've arrived."

We approach the two-story structure and ascend the wooden steps. A guard at the door stops us and asks for identification and credentials.

AR steps in front of me confidently, flashing a smile at the guard. "We are here to conduct maintenance on the units in this building. I am AR-6180, and this is my partner, HE-2102."

I'm impressed at how easily he slips into the lie and how earnest and truthful he sounds. I'd almost believe him if I didn't know what we came here to do. His polite and self-assured smile never wavering, he shows the guard his badge and places a hand on my shoulder to push me past him. He does this in one smooth action, never taking his eyes off the guard.

Said guard is so preoccupied with AR's performance, he doesn't seem to notice me walking through. That is, until the door beeps.

The guard whips around, his expression morphing from shock, to confusion, to rage. "Put your hands up!"

AR mutters a curse under his breath, his friendly facade falling off his face to expose a wince. I don't waste any time letting the guard radio anyone. I shove him in the gut hard, and he crashes to the ground. The back of his head smacks the wooden floorboards of the porch, and he passes out. AR eyes me warily, then nudges me back inside, despite the beep. He steps gingerly over the unconscious soldier's body.

"He's the father of someone I know," AR says, glancing at the guard. "Oh, well. Let us just hope we don't get into any more trouble than we are now."

"Sorry," I mutter, not at all apologetic.

"No, it's my fault. I totally forgot the detectors on the door. We should hurry."

I raise an eyebrow at that, but I don't dwell on it. He's picked up a new, subtle urgency, which would set me off if not for the direness of the situation. Perhaps he was more affected by my attack on the guard than he let on, not as if that's my problem.

AR rushes to the desk. He leans over it and grabs a ring of keys. He motions to a door around the front desk, opens it, and ushers me into the hallway.

We break into one of the first rooms. AR switches on the lights to reveal racks of coats identical to his, as well as boots and gloves. To my utter disappointment, the room holds no weapons or food, but at least we're going one step in the right direction.

Or two steps, I think as my eyes lock on to a wide glass pane on the opposite end of the room. Behind the window is a cot set up near a dark wood table. Sitting on the table is none other than HG.

Relief and warmth rise in my chest, but I chalk it up to gratitude for the convenience.

HG's staring at the window but she doesn't notice us—doesn't see us. It must be one-way; there were many interrogation rooms like this back in the Evil buildings.

There's a panel in the wall to the left of the window, most likely the entrance to the cell.

"Why's she here?" I ask as I sort through white uniforms and jackets.

"She's in for an interrogation."

"No, duh." I exchange my ragged boots for the warmer Kaltic ones and slip on a coat with a fluffy lining. "What is this place exactly?"

"A militia designated building." He's leaning in the doorway with a careful expression, watching me pocket a pair of gloves for later.

"Right." I frown. "Open her cell door."

"What?" He blinks.

I flash a sharp smile. "I'm having an interrogation. Open the door."

The threat goes unsaid, but he's smart enough to know that it's an order and not a suggestion. Crossing the room calmly, AR fits one of the keys into a slot in the panel and the door to the cell swings open.

HG glances up, and her pale green eyes widen. She's perched with her legs folded on top of the table, but at our entry, she slides off and folds her arms.

I cock an eyebrow.

A grin tugs at the corners of her mouth. "Travis."

# Chapter VII

## —Jack—

## Change of Plans

I search for Nora with my mind. I try to remember what she looks like, how tall she is, the last conversation I had with her. The thread appears, and the darkness turns to light.

I'm in a city, standing on a roof. It's not familiar. It's too warm here, and the buildings are in near ruins, reduced to crumbling walls and iron framework. Nora's there too, curled up under a thin blanket, sleeping under the open night sky. Next to her is a flickering lantern and a large backpack. I walk over to her and shake her shoulder, watching as her gray eyes flutter open. It's just a dream, but normally I have to wake the person's mind, take them out of their dream into my own scenic land.

The moonlight blankets us, mingling with the lantern's light. The rest of the city is a soupy darkness, enveloped in shadows cast by the tall buildings that tamper with the moon's bleached glow.

"Jack," Nora mutters, sitting up. "Did you need something?"

"Yeah," I say more aggressively than intended. "How come you didn't tell us you were leaving?"

She frowns. "I left a letter, didn't I?"

"I mean in person."

"Oh." She sighs. "It's too complicated. You guys wouldn't have let me leave otherwise. Or you'd try to come with me and get yourselves in trouble."

"Where are you?" I ask, gesturing vaguely to the landscape. "This isn't our city. I didn't make this place up."

Rather than respond, she gazes at the inky horizon of the dreamscape.

"Nora," I say.

She seems lost in thought, her brow furrowed in concentration.

"*Nora,*" I repeat.

She flinches. "Hm?"

"Where are you now?"

"Don't come after me, Jack," she says, her voice dropping in a warning.

"You're not the boss of me," I tell her childishly. "I want to help you."

"No," she growls.

"Why not? Are you in trouble?" My concern level is rising.

"No. I'm on a mission."

"To find Travis?"

Her eyes flash in exasperation. "No. His case is too uncertain, but I know he's alive. That's all."

I blink. "How do you know?"

"I have other matters to attend to," she snaps, then exhales.

I tilt my head. "I thought … Wait, you didn't answer my question. How do you know he's okay?"

She looks away. "He told me."

"Scratch that," I say. "Are *you* okay?"

"I'm serious, Jack," Nora hisses. "I don't know how, but when I left this morning, I suddenly recalled a memory of Travis telling me that he wasn't dead, that he was sorting out an issue, and once he did, he'd come looking for me."

I stare at her as she chuckles bitterly.

"He's such a liar," she says, glaring into the distance. "Always has been, but he should know better than to lie to me. There's something going on, but I don't have the resources or the abilities right now to find him."

"Wait, wait," I interrupt. "You got this all from a memory? Like, from your childhood, or—"

"No, it was recent." She pinches the bridge of her nose. "Before he disappeared. It's— It's hard to explain really; it gets fuzzier the more I think about it, but the information's still there. I must have overlooked it then, but thinking back on it, he had to be referring to the future, or our present timeline now."

My eyebrows furrow. "How can that happen? Travis can't see into the future, can he?"

She shakes her head. "No, he … I don't know, but I know someone who could have an idea."

"What do you mean?"

"I'm going to find Cole," she says.

"Huh?" I'm completely caught off guard. "Isn't he at the main building? You could just come back and wait for the next shipment."

"He left the Indifferents' base three weeks ago. I'll be honest, Jack, you've been kind of oblivious lately," she says.

I recall dinner, when I learned the Captain's name. Alistair. Am I really absentminded like Nora says? Thomas didn't know his name either, and he's ten different kinds of attentive.

"Why did Cole leave? Where did he go?" I ask instead.

"No one seems to know, though that's nothing unusual. But I have a hunch where he went. I talked to him a lot before the first shipments, since he visited your camp to take notes. I think he's working on some sort of secret project," she explains. "I'm going to help him. And I bet he knows how to locate Travis, too."

Nora's words settle in my mind, turning over and over. Secret project? Cole's the one who made the stone. Is he trying to make another one? And the way Nora said "your camp" like she never belonged.

I inhale slowly.

Nora gets up. "It's time for me to go."

"Nora, wait—"

"Jack," she says, facing me again. "Stay safe. Take care of everyone. I'll make sure to find you after I complete my mission."

"Nora—"

But then she turns her back, steps to the edge of the roof and jumps off, waking herself up and leaving me alone in a dark and empty city.

I sit on the ledge of the building, feeling hollow inside. Nora's officially gone. And I'm stuck here, stuck at camp.

It's no longer a what-if question. From what Nora said, Travis must be in some sort of trouble. She may not have the abilities to find him, but I might. If I can get more information based on what I already know from my various dreams, I can come up with a plan to reach Travis. Nora thinks something's going on, and beyond my own loyalty, I also want to figure it out. This could be bigger than just Travis.

I need a plan, but I can't wait for the Indifferents, or Nora for that matter. I must take matters into my own hands because no one else can. I will find Travis.

Until morning reaches me.

# Chapter VIII

## —Travis—

## Free

HG walks toward us, excitement playing in her bright eyes. I step back, not wanting her to encroach on my personal space so suddenly. AR is silent as he moves behind me to lean on the wall next to the doorframe.

"Nice outfit," HG comments, her gaze running over my borrowed clothing with mild curiosity and amusement.

"Thanks," I mutter, stuffing my hands along with the stone in my pockets and trying to focus.

AR said this is a militia designated base, leaving me to wonder if all their bases had interrogation rooms as well as armories and the like. The building I was held in seemed to only consist of the cells and the main area where the soldiers milled about.

I look back at AR and catch him glancing out the door. Although he's not doing anything suspicious, my gut instinct is sinking lower and lower. I don't want to assume the worst about a potential ally, though I'm not putting too much faith in him either. I know all too well how dangerous it is to trust people right away, especially in an unknown environment.

"… had to drag you back to the city walls, and then they took you," HG continues, and it takes me a second to realize she's been talking to me. "How did you get here, anyway?"

"I broke out of my cell. AR brought me here to get supplies, and we knocked out the guard," I summarize.

"Supplies?"

"Correction," AR intercedes. "*You* knocked out the soldier. I simply did my job and escorted you here."

"Thanks," I mutter. "In that case, you're still my hostage."

"AR … Hostage?" HG echoes. "Wait, what are you talking about?"

AR shrugs. "Voluntary compliance."

"Sure, whatever," I snip. "HG, how long has it been since we arrived here?"

She frowns. "Perhaps twelve hours or so."

"Alright, and how long did it take you to get to the city?"

She scoffs. "Lugging you around? A few hours."

"Yes, thank you," I grumble. "Won't happen next time, I assure you."

"Next time?" AR parrots. "HG-8057, you're not planning on fleeing Kaltic again, are you?"

"Mm, perhaps. Is that a problem?" she says. "You are a soldier, and yet, here you are, accompanying an outsider. What is it you want?"

His eyes widen just a fraction. "I— Well, there's nothing I really *want*. I'm just curious. It's not that I want to leave Kaltic or betray my militia at all. I respect the Light, and Kaltic and its rules. But now I know there is something beyond Kaltic."

"There is," I say, stepping in. "Remember I told you about the cities and ports? And the people—there's so many people. You'd find it hard to believe with the kind of conditions we have out there, but we're surviving."

I ramble on about the outside world, hoping AR will be intrigued enough to continue helping me for good. If he makes up his mind like HG, I'll have two reliable allies who want the same thing as me. To get out.

“I know,” HG breathes, her green eyes sparkling. “If only I could make it past the blizzards and mountains, I could find them.”

AR stares at us contemplatively, his crystal-blue eyes dark and murky. “So, HG-8057, you really intend to go back out there?”

She nods. “Travis is all the proof I need now. Before, I blindly fled Kaltic hoping I’d find something. After all, the outsiders we’ve gotten before had to come from somewhere. But they always disappeared after we intercepted them, and I never got the answers I wanted. Now, I have living evidence of a world out there. So I’ll help Travis.”

He falters, suddenly looking more conflicted than I’ve seen him in my short time in his nonchalant presence. I watch both of them silently, opting to leave this to them now, while I try to shape a rocky plan with the infinitesimal amount of information I have.

“Say, Travis,” AR starts, his clear gaze flicking to me.

“Yes?”

“Are there rules to the outside world? Are there laws? Punishments? Names? Tell me, Travis, are you free?”

I stare back at him, unsure of how to respond. What a stupidly easy question. Am I free? That should be obvious. Of course I am. But am I really, when most everyone is a slave to something? People long for power, control, the world, and it ends up ruling them.

“In the outside world,” I begin, “you have freedom. You have the power to choose. And part of that choice is whether you’ll keep that freedom or toss it away. You can either live freely, or you can be chained to something. You can let things, people, circumstances, put you in a cage.

You can cater to the world, and you'll never be free. But you can always choose. And right now, I choose to be free."

# Chapter IX

## —Jack—

## **Repeat**

I'm awake before everyone, fifteen minutes before the wake-up call, according to the clock. I can't go back to sleep, not after what just happened with Nora. Too many thoughts whirl through my mind as usual, and I don't know how to connect them.

I try to piece together the risks and benefits of both leaving and staying. There's the matter of Thala and the Indifferents. I don't know if she'll let me leave to look for Travis, and the next shipment is still a few weeks away. That's the only time I'll get to see her, and the Indifferents for that matter. With their power, I'd never get a chance to go. But if I leave, I have to take my friends into account.

I know Thomas will follow me no matter what. The thought hits me with more prickly waves of guilt, but I try to shake it off. It's Thomas's choice. I'll make more of an effort to be aware of his feelings. I can't change the past, but I can change myself for the future.

Then there's Cali. She doesn't have a mother, and her father works in a leadership position like the Captain. I've never met her dad, and she never talks about him like they're close. Still, I can't assume she'll want to go on another expedition with me, so I'll have to talk to her as well.

I need more opinions. Thomas had a good point, but Nora confirmed Travis is alive. I can't sit around and do nothing if he needs us.

The lights flicker on, and I hear the low mumbles of the other boys stirring as their minds adjust to the waking world. Sitting up in my bunk, I stretch and scrub at my eyes, kicking the thin blanket off my legs.

"Good morning!" The Captain's voice cuts through the air. "Get up and dressed for work!"

Amid a few groans and lethargic mutters, we all get up, fold our blankets, and prepare for the day.

I pull on a long-sleeved shirt and grab my coat, putting it on as I walk to the bathroom to brush my teeth. My messy reflection stares back at me, dark circles under my hazel eyes. I rip my gaze away from the cracked mirror, which was a new installment from the Indifferents, and shoulder my bag. My canteen hangs on a clip on the strap, still filled with water I saved from the kitchen.

One of the older Scavengers passes out jerky to keep us sustained for the day. As the bag of food drops into my hand, major *déjà vu* rocks my vision. It's exactly the same as it was before the battle. Nothing has changed at all. How can these people live their lives in repetition? Then I realize I used to do that too. Every day since I got a job, I'd get up, go to work, eat, sleep, and repeat, and I thought nothing of it. Sure, some days were better or worse than others, and I had a few highlights, but other than that, everything was the same.

Only, it can't be the same. Not since the stone and the battle. Not since Travis disappeared.

As I walk down the hall where the others are waiting to be released, I see the Captain and another adult talking in low tones by the wall. While I don't want to eavesdrop, something the Captain says catches my interest.

"… going to leave the camp," he murmurs. "Things will move on without me, but I have to find them again."

I blink, then hop around the wall into another hallway so I'm out of sight but within earshot.

"They're back in that radiation station, yeah?" the other adult muses. "It's farther south."

"Mhm. Not as far south as the City, though. Definitely not as cold."

"Well, I wish you luck in finding them," the other adult says. "Where will you go after?"

"I'm not sure. Maybe go down to the southern port?"

"No way. It's freezing around there. And way too close to the City. Why would you go there?"

"Yvonne stayed around there," the Captain says. "Last I heard of her, she was doing well. I might just try to live there, too."

I stop listening and mull over his words. The Captain's planning on leaving? He mentioned going south, and that it's cold there. Cold, like in my dream when I tried searching for Travis. It could be a coincidence, but there aren't many places that are freezing. From what I've learned by talking to other adults or listening in on stories of my parents' scouting adventures, the farther south you get, the colder it is.

I wonder if the Captain plans to make an announcement that he's going. If he's heading into the cold, to a place he's familiar with, he might know something about the location from my dreams.

"Jackie, you okay?" Nico's voice shakes me out of my thoughts.

I keep forgetting I can't accidentally broadcast anymore, so people can't easily tell whenever I have an issue or when I'm spying on unsuspecting adults. It's nice knowing my thoughts are private. Ever since the battle, my progress with keeping them that way has become more involuntary and natural.

"Yeah," I answer quickly. "I'm fine. Is it time now?"

"Yup," he says. "C'mon, I'll walk you guys there."

I nod, following the group through the familiar yet confusing tunnels to the same old trapdoor that leads to the roof, where I last saw Travis.

It puzzles me what exactly happened to him. I'm sure he died at the end of the battle, but then his body disappeared. Nora once suggested that the stone had the ability to heal, but Travis himself shot down that idea quickly. I remember Travis's last words clearly, reminding us it wasn't the end. And later, a memory, a whisper.

*"Indigo. Faded."* It had to be some sort of code, or a fragmented message.

The probability that Travis died just doesn't add up, especially with the information I got from Nora.

The Scavengers disperse, running in different directions like they rehearsed it. I shoulder my bag and leap off the roof to the next one, not stopping until I'm forced to climb down into an alley when the buildings are too far apart.

I look around, absent-mindedly twisting the stone on my wrist. It's thinner since I gave a chunk of it to Travis. But he faded from existence. Or so was the thought. Nora knows he's alive, and I want to prove her right by finding him.

Still, leaving on a whim is reckless and dangerous. I need to organize an ideal plan instead of rushing blindly to the nearest available source, like I did when my friends and I escaped camp and found the Indifferents. It was risky then, even if it turned out alright. However, with our lives potentially on the line if I do go, I need to be more cautious.

*What would Nora do?* She left with only a note as her final word. I'm definitely not going to do that.

I walk along the backstreets and pick up pieces of metal and bricks. Bricks that are in good condition are useful and are in high demand from the camp. My bag gets heavier and heavier. Despite not being out lately, I haven't lost my athleticism. I'm not tired yet from lugging my bag around the city. I've always preferred moving around out here because of the freedom and the breath of crisp air.

Swiping a loose hair from my face, I sit down inside an empty building to eat and drink. Sitting in the dark with just the stone and a little light from the empty spaces where doors and windows are supposed to be is relaxing, but it reminds me of how lonely it is to be by myself.

I rearrange my pack to fit more stuff before I walk back out into the gray sunlight. My decision lies on my shoulders, but I'm not scared. When it comes to the people I care about, I can't be.

Thomas's earlier points about the dangers of leaving are valid, but that doesn't make them right if Travis is alive but not here. Last I saw him, he was dead. If he's alive, there's no way he can be perfectly alright, physically. After all, he was shot and died just a few minutes later. If he's caught up somewhere, somewhere bad enough he wouldn't want Nora to go—bad enough that he'd lie to her about it—then he must be in danger. I haven't known Travis for long, but he became a part of the family when he joined us on our first expedition. He saved us numerous times, and he sacrificed himself for one of us. It's a given that I won't let him try to brave it alone.

Whether with my friends or not, I'm going to find Travis. I have to. If I learned anything since the battle, it's that the world is big, but family is bigger.

A plan starts to form in my mind, hidden and trapped in my head. I realize I can't be impulsive as I piece together fragments of an idea, incorporating my friends, the farewells, and the little information I have: from my dreams, the conversation with Nora, and what I heard from the Captain. I have to talk to him more, too. But after I set everything up back at camp, I'll be ready.

I'm going to bring my friends home.

# Chapter X

## —Travis—

## **Control**

AR stares at us for a few seconds as if thinking over what I just said, processing it as he leans against the cell wall. He blinks and pushes himself off the wall to stand in front of us.

"Suit yourself," AR says blandly, his mouth drawn into a thin line.

And then that line cracks, twisting upward into a smile. The bad feeling drops in my stomach, the dread settling with cold resolve.

"I'm amazed how long I was able to stall you," AR muses with an unsettling smirk.

"What do you mean?" HG's eyes are wide with confusion.

"You really think I'm joining you just like that?" The pity in his voice is like poison as he looks at me. He lets out a huff of laughter. "You're one of the touched, Travis, and your 'freedom' is tainted. Just look at you."

He waves his hand at me, and my eyes track the motion. In his fingers is a device—probably one of those radios. The pieces click together the more he goes on. He led me to where HG was held, which happened to be an interrogation building with the things I needed, both to buy time for his militia to ambush me in a new building and to lock me in. The destination was a ploy. Now that the militia is back in the game, they will call for help from whatever they were trying to signal before. The Axe, or something.

Whatever that may be, I'm not looking forward to coming into contact with it, especially if it's their last line of defense.

Overall, I can't believe how stupid I am.

"You're betraying him?" HG mutters in disbelief. "I thought you were on board. Voluntary compliance."

AR glances at her. "Travis said it himself; I'm just a hostage. For someone who is so sure of Kaltic's flaws while everyone else is 'blind,' you really are naïve. I am a soldier. I am loyal to this city." His focus drifts away from her face as he talks, his gaze resting just above her shoulder. "I'm not following your delusion on a whim, and I'm not helping an outsider because of his pretentious 'freedom.'"

I turn away from AR, my mind working furiously to combat and outsmart his plan. I should have known better than to let my guard down around him, to assume he'd want to help me just because I offered a concept he can't understand. HG was already on my side before I came here. She always wanted to leave.

The stone flashes in my hand, and the familiar click of a gun sounds as I point it at his face. "I suppose now that I'm with HG, I don't need you anymore."

His blue eyes stare at me head-on, and he doesn't flinch when I take a step forward.

"I'm impressed," I continue. "Really, I am. But you still served your purpose. Thanks, AR."

"You have nowhere to run," he states. "They will be here soon."

"Mm, maybe." I wave the gun nonchalantly, then look at HG. "Meet me outside on this side of the building. No one's here yet to stop you. Go. Close the door on your way out."

She nods without a question, and heads for the open door. AR reaches to grab her. I move between them and use my unarmed hand to block his. HG dashes out into the hallway and shoves the metal door shut until it clicks, locked. I can hear her faint footsteps as she flees the building.

A dangerous spark glints in AR's eyes as he lunges for me, ducking under my gun arm. I brace myself as he tackles me, aiming for my stomach. The pain from my wound rises back up like a fire. Bringing my elbow down, I clock him in the head and knee him in the chest. He stumbles back.

The stone reverts to a bracelet as I swing around and kick him in the shoulder hard enough to overbalance him. Leaping over him as he falls, I charge at the wall opposite the door and fade. My body passes through the gray concrete.

I make sure I keep my eyesight while fading so I know when I'm outside. Focusing specifically on one of my senses while using my ability is tiring, but luckily there's only one layer of wall to pass through, so I'm able to release my ability reflex the moment I'm out.

HG's outside, waiting in the shadow of the building. I stop fading and skid to a halt beside her. She stares at me in shock.

"What?" I grunt, holding my stomach and gritting my teeth.

"Nothing," she says quickly. "We should go. Are you alright?"

"Fine."

"You need medical attention. You're bleeding."

"It's like that," I say, waving her off because I don't have time to worry about my wound. "We need to do something to stall the militia so we have time to run."

"Like what?"

I back up beside her and pat my pockets, the natural habit of having tools on me at all times reflecting in my instinctive movements. I only have the gloves and the stone. Figuring that should suffice with its many capabilities, I turn to HG.

"What happens in Kaltic if a building is on fire?" I ask.

HG eyes me warily. "The militia will put out the fire."

"How long does that take?"

"An hour or two? It depends on the fire."

The stone flashes on my wrist, molding into a lighter in my hand. I step toward the building and flick the lighter on. A white flame burns a scarlet red at the base.

"Travis?" HG says hesitantly. "AR is still in there—"

"I'm aware."

"He's locked in there."

"He has the keys."

Without another word, I jog around the side of the building, keeping low to the ground and close to the wall, hoping my white clothes blend in.

I don't hear or see the militia, but I know AR wasn't lying when he said they were coming soon. I need to be fast.

Dashing around the front, I see the guard is already gone, another reminder that the militia won't be far behind me.

All the more reason to commit arson.

I walk up the steps and crouch by the wooden railing of the porch. I'm not sure how effective stone-fire is, especially in the winter, but the porch isn't too damp. I doubt the fire will spread far inside since the rest of the building is concrete, and the porch itself is wide. If I want to stall them, I have to set as much ablaze as possible.

I find a spot to start the fire. Flicking the lighter on, I lower the glowing purple tool to the wood. Surprisingly, it flares up on the first try. I duck through the beeping detector, setting all the flammable and easily accessible things I can see alight. I bolt back onto the porch and ignite different areas of the wood, and lastly, the stairs. The odd chemical smell of the fire grows stronger with the flames. I scramble off the porch and run. No time to supervise the crime.

"What did you do?" HG asks the second I return. I can already see smoke rising, even from behind the wall.

I shake my head. "I'll tell you on the way. Let's move."

"Right, sorry. Come on."

"Wait," I call, my boots skidding as I abruptly stop behind her.

"Yes?"

I inhale slowly. "Look, we need to organize a plan of escape before we start running around. Right now, we need a map."

"Perhaps we can find one in the Light's office," HG decides. "He's the leader of Kaltic; he may have what you're looking for. But we need to avoid him."

"We can check there first, then. If he's not in, we'll sneak in and out," I suggest.

"Right," she says. "If we do encounter him, just know he won't willingly help you."

"Sure," I say.

She nods and motions for me to follow. We veer off the side street toward what I assume is the center of the city, judging by the smaller surrounding walls.

We dart around a building and into an adjacent alley. I wonder briefly how close the militia is and how big the fire is now, and whether I knocked AR unconscious when he fell. I doubt it. My mind jumps to future situations: he alerts the militia that I've escaped again with HG while they're worrying about the fire. They might send a different group to look for us. I'm glad they don't know where we're headed.

I plot out different scenarios as we go along, individual plans for anything that can go wrong. But I can't be completely prepared because I have barely any information on Kaltic.

There's a bend in the road and taller steel buildings come into view. Even from ground level, I can see them rise and glisten against the winter sunlight. The area we're heading into is more urban compared to the streets I walked around with AR to get to HG.

It's at this moment that I am able to process the sheer vastness of Kaltic. It's huge. I haven't seen any civilians—the streets are empty—but they have to be somewhere. From what I've gathered of Kaltic, the city is organized. It has its own militia and separate holding centers, and the streets are cleared of snow.

I glance behind us, and I'm alarmed to see clouds of smoke, leaving me to wonder how badly the building is burning.

"So what did you do?" HG asks, her voice soft, her gaze lined up with mine.

I keep my voice quiet too. It feels like if the silence hears us, we'll be swallowed by it. "Set the wood on fire."

"Excuse me?"

"AR will be fine. I doubt the fire will go inside. Concrete isn't flammable."

She nods briskly. "Right. Are you going to be—"

"Yes, I can manage," I say, exhaling and trying to keep pace, even though my abdomen burns.

"Travis, do you really need this map?" she asks, her eyes narrowed in concern.

"Yes," I say. "It's my ticket out of here. I just need to locate where I am and get out of the city. There are ports and checkpoints all over the world. Even if Kaltic is in the middle of nowhere, there has to be a way to get back to the outside world. So yeah, I really need that map."

She hums. "I see."

"Why?"

"If you get caught, I don't know what will happen to you." Her voice is solemn. "And I need you."

I frown, though I know what she means. In reality, we need each other. She's useful to me because she knows her way around Kaltic. I'm crucial to her because I'm from the outside world and know how to navigate it.

"Then I won't get caught," I say firmly.

"Right."

"Over there!" Pounding footsteps follow the shout.

*Of course.*

HG yanks my sleeve and pulls me into the nearest alley.

"Outsider! HG-8057! Stay where you are with your hands up," a rough voice shouts.

"That was fast," I mutter. "Maybe I should set another building on fire."

"I can't tell if you're trying to be humorous, but this isn't funny," HG hisses. We're crammed into the narrow space between the two buildings.

"Any ideas?" I ask. None of mine are too great. Or safe.

"We need to lose them," she growls. "But how? They shouldn't be armed—they would have taken longer to get those kinds of weapons—but I'm not sure. Can you see?"

Hugging the wall, I edge around the corner and take a quick glance out. There are about five soldiers and the leader I met before. Like I thought, they split up to deal with us and the fire simultaneously.

I recount the details to HG, adding that I didn't notice any weapons, which strikes me as odd. But that's better for me, and I'm not one to question a good thing.

"There was no one else, right?" she asks. "Not a woman with, uh, short black hair who's carrying a very large, very sharp weapon?"

I shake my head. "I saw all of those people back at the base where I woke up."

"So the Axe hasn't gotten here yet," she mutters to herself. "She must be on the other side of the city in public transit."

"That's good?"

"Yes. If there's six of them in total, do you think you could fight them?"

I purse my lips, my hand instinctually hovering over my abdomen. "If all of them fight like AR, then no. Even with my weapon, it'd be difficult. And I don't want to make a mess."

She exhales slowly.

"I'll go out there," I say anyway, twirling the stone. It shifts into a gun in my hand.

"What are you going to do?" she asks, alarmed.

"Not sure yet. I'll wing it."

"No—"

"We don't have a lot of time," I say. "I have to do something."

"But—"

"Just trust me. Wait here."

Taking a deep breath, I run from the alley into the street, transforming the stone back into an actual stone.

"Halt!" the woman yells.

I turn to face her group, schooling my expression to one I'd use when dealing with an enemy team.

"There aren't a lot of you," I note as I step toward them.

They all stand their ground, but they're stiff. Most likely they've never had a threat quite like me.

"Stay right where you are," the woman growls.

"Don't you want me to turn myself in?" I say with mock-innocence, continuing to walk to them.

"I will not repeat myself."

I use the closing distance to scrutinize my opponents, read their body language, and check for anything suspicious on them. The woman has a metal device in her hand that I hadn't counted as a weapon, but I can't be sure. It could be another radio or something akin to a taser.

"We can do this the easy way or the hard way," I say with false bravado, not entirely sure where I'm going with this. "Easy way: you let me go. Hard way: I take all of you out."

"You're wounded," the woman says. "Even if you did defeat us, you wouldn't escape in time. The Axe is on her way."

"Don't underestimate me." I let venom drip into my words. I'm still advancing.

Her eyes narrow, and her hand clenches around the device. A creeping sense of urgency and dread crawls up my throat as I begin to believe the thing is a stun gun.

I hold up the stone. "You know what this is? You probably don't. I noticed the marks around my wrist when I woke up, so I assume you were trying to get it off me. Bad idea. You know why?"

My eyes follow her hand as it slowly rises.

"Because this thing is *touched*," I continue. "Just holding it in your hand can cause you to become touched permanently. Maybe even just being near it."

The soldiers behind the woman glance at each other, clear discomfort on their faces.

"You're bluffing," the woman says. "There have been no effects from that rock."

"Oh, not immediately, no," I say, raising my eyebrows. "But maybe. Would you like to find out?"

"What do you—"

I charge, looking into the eyes of a soldier behind the woman, and throw the stone. "Catch!"

I saw Jack do this back at his camp in the battle, and the memory is in the forefront of my mind.

The soldier instinctively catches the stone despite his expression of horror. The others turn to look at him, the panic in their eyes matching his. Just as AR did to me, I use this distraction to duck under the woman's arm and tackle her.

She sucks in a breath at the impact of my knee in her stomach, and I roll away. The soldiers start shouting, and the one who caught the stone yelps and drops it, his reaction delayed.

I snatch up the stone as I kick one of the soldiers in the calves before getting up. In their panic, they're not able to attack me like AR did, which I use to my advantage. Two are on the ground while the other four back away from me, fear etched into their faces.

I've taken on more opponents at the same time than this, and a good portion of my life was spent fighting. With the Evils, I learned to understand and memorize body language, which helped me mimic the techniques of enemies and use it against them. But the soldiers aren't attacking. If I try charging, I'll be easily surrounded.

"Come at me!" I hiss, the stone flashing into a dagger in my hand.

A couple of them do, stupidly brave. The other three try to help their leader. I click my tongue and square my shoulders, then sidestep the first one who comes at me, using my free hand to forcefully push her to the ground. She stumbles and falls into the snow.

The other one tries to grab me from the side, but I arc my knife around and he jumps back. I kick out my foot as he dodges, tripping him, then crouch over him and sock him in the jaw. His head smacks against the pavement and he's out cold. I shed my coat to maneuver better without the constricting padding, holding the clothing by the elbows.

Huffing, I sprint over to where the other four are, ducking under the first one's arm and whipping the coat out so it slaps against his face, effectively blinding him long enough for me to shove him to the ground. The other one swings her fist at my face, which I block with my arm. Shaking off the thudding pain, I grab her arm and yank her to the side. She goes crashing into the ground next to her partner.

I'm not feeling too bad at this point, glad that I haven't lost my touch, when a jolt rips into my calf. All the muscles there contract, and my knees buckle. I try to catch my fall by stepping to the side with my other foot, but I stumble.

With my palm flat against the ground, I try to push myself up, but everything burns and tingles and stings. Instead I roll onto my back and look up to see the woman with the device in her hand. It crackles, the electricity buzzing on its short metal tongs.

Cursing, I kick away from her as she lunges for me. I feel my eyes widen as a shadow rises over me.

Then the lady jerks away from me, landing in the snow. Above me stands HG, her fist still clenched.

"I—" My words die in my throat.

"Are you alright?" she asks. Three of the soldiers are missing and the rest are unconscious.

"Yeah," I mumble, rolling to my knees. The effects of the shock have already worn off.

She holds out her hand. "Let's go before anyone finds them here."

"Right." I take her hand and she pulls me up. "Thanks."

"We need to go to the Capital building to get to the Light's office," HG says, dusting her clothes off. "We just need to make sure we don't do anything to disturb the rest of the city. We can't have the machines of Kaltic rise. They aren't so easy to deal with."

I swallow, somewhat less confident at the mention of machines. But I've made it this far, and with HG's help, I can do it. I will escape Kaltic.

# Chapter XI

## —Jack—

## **Quick Decision**

My bag is heavy as I make my way back to camp. It tugs downward on my shoulders, the contents inside knocking together as I jump across roofs. Despite everything that's going on—Nora gone, Travis's whereabouts still unknown, and the new tension on my friendship with Thomas—I'm strangely calm. My head is clear, and I'm not fretting so much. It's an odd sensation not to worry over everything. Somehow, with each step, with each jump, my nervous thoughts loosen up. And then they're gone.

I no longer think about what might happen later; my mind dwells on the present.

I land back at camp at the same time as a couple of other Scavengers. We greet each other and make our way down the hatch. Nico is there, waiting as usual. It's refreshing to see him after being by myself all day, but it reminds me that I have to leave him later, if my unhatched plan goes accordingly. I choose not to think about that right now.

"How're you doing?" I ask him casually.

"Eh," he answers, his green eyes dull with boredom. "What did you get?"

I smile. "Nothing special, but I did find a cool-looking feather."

His expression brightens with excitement. "Can I see?"

I show him the feather, black, soft, and glossy. It's large, probably from a crow of some sort. Nicholas rubs his thumb over it.

"'S cool," he agrees. "Can I keep it?"

"Sure, bud."

I walk alongside him toward the Long Room. The parts of my plan pop back up in my mind, minus any anxiety. I feel more like a spring coil, packed with intense energy, waiting to fly.

"Hey, Nico," I say, dumping the contents of my bag carefully into a bin for the collectors.

"Yeah?"

"You know where Mom and Dad are?"

"They left a few hours ago," he replies, glancing away.

"Oh."

So much for that confrontation. But it's alright, I can salvage the rest of my plan easily.

"Well," I sigh, "too bad I didn't get to see them off. Were you able to?"

Nico hums. "Yeah."

I falter. He doesn't seem too concerned or as sad as I thought he would be. He just looks resigned, the bright sparkle in his eyes replaced with a calm and quiet light. He seems older, like something in him has shifted from the little kid I always knew to someone who reminds me more of me when I was his age, with our parents gone for weeks on end. It's not something I want to see reflected in him.

"How long is it until dinner?" I ask as we walk down a corridor in need of lighting maintenance.

"Forty minutes," he says softly.

I raise my eyebrows. "Want to go exploring?"

"I already know where everything is."

"Well, yes, but I don't. And there are different people in different places every day," I tell him, hoping my voice is cheery enough to ignite that playful energy he always had. "Let's look around."

His pensive expression cracks into a small smile. "Okay. Follow me."

For someone who's lived in the same building most of my memorable life, I don't have much of a grasp on it. Nico takes me down to the first level, which is oddly vacant, aside from the stacks of boxes near the front of the room and outside the entrance of the building. I've never gone in or out through here. I always exit and enter from the roof.

Next, we go to the basement where the boiler room is. The people down there greet Nico by name. At this point, I don't doubt he knows everyone in this building.

On the second floor we run into Cali. She's helping move furniture and crates onto carts. She waves hello to us before turning to lift a couple of boxes using her ability, MindLift. Nico tugs at my sleeve, meaning it's time to move on.

It's refreshing to spend time with him, since I rarely see him between our two jobs. It reminds me of when we were both younger, exploring the tunnels and getting lost, though we always managed to find our way back with his ability. Thomas would join us on our expeditions, and when Cali became friends with us, she would too.

Those adventures were the most fun I ever had, and it makes me wonder if traveling with all of them again would really be so bad. Dangerous, yes, but together we're unstoppable.

***

When dinner rolls around, I catch Thomas and Cali in the line. Nico already has his food and he's sitting with his own friends, but I decide to wait for mine.

Thomas eyes me carefully, studying my face. Even though my thoughts are now private, he still knows what I'm thinking.

"Okay, okay," I mutter, knowing his expression is the one he makes when he wants an answer but doesn't want to ask directly. "I made up my mind, and I'm going."

With a long-suffering sigh, Thomas rubs his forehead. "Have you come up with something that even remotely resembles a plan?"

Cali cocks an eyebrow. "What're you talking about? Don't tell me you two are scheming something without me. How rude."

A smile graces Thomas's lips. "We're not."

She huffs. "You're lying and I want in."

I hold up my hands placatingly. "This was my idea. Uh, anyway, I'm leaving."

"Well, duh," is Cali's response. "When are we going?"

"We need to get packed tonight," I say, lowering my voice. "So we have the chance to leave at any given time."

"Sounds sneaky," Cali comments.

The line moves up, and we're able to get our food and settle at a table near one of the doors. The chatter in the Dining Hall is merely background noise to the thoughts bouncing around my head. Knowing my friends are going through with this is both reassuring and worrying. If anything happens to us, I'm responsible.

"So, what's the plan?" Thomas asks, setting down his tray.

I inhale slowly. "I haven't told you about my dreams, right?"

They both shake their heads.

"Well, I've been searching for Travis," I explain. "In my dreams. There's— There isn't a connection, but I have been having these weird dreams of a place I've never seen. Like this open field, but it's just *snow*. And rock. As well as buildings, like a city. And it's colder than anything. Colder than here. I usually wake up after a few minutes with a migraine, but I think there's meaning behind those visions. They have to relate to Travis."

Cali sits forward. "How come you never mentioned this before?"

I shrug. "I didn't really think anything of it until I met with Nora in a dream recently, and then later overheard the Captain talking about something."

Thomas hums in acknowledgment, and Cali raises her eyebrows. "Do tell."

"So, Nora said Travis sent her a message through a memory," I try to explain. "She basically confirmed he's alive, but he could be in trouble. Nora's off looking for Cole now, since apparently he's gone too. She said he'd have more of a lead on Travis's whereabouts. But I heard the Captain speaking with one of his friends earlier. He plans on leaving. And he said he'll be going down south. I don't remember much else from what they were saying, but whatever he means by south, he means he's going where it's freezing."

"So you think he may be talking about the same place as your dream," Thomas sums up.

"Pretty much, yeah."

"What are the odds of that?" he asks.

I shrug. "I'll have to talk to him. Otherwise, my only evidence is trusting that when they say 'cold,' they mean really freezing. Like year-round snow. According to the maps, the south is the only area like that."

"Do you know when he plans on leaving?" Cali asks.

I shake my head. "I'll try to confront him tonight, but until then, we need to be prepared. We need to leave as soon as possible if we want to make it before the Indifferents' next shipment, since they definitely won't let us go, and judging from how Nora was acting, Travis may not have that long."

"We'll be ready by tonight, then," Cali clarifies, and Thomas just exhales and nods. "You give us the word and we'll meet up here, at the Hall, since we all know our way here. From there, I guess we'll just have to wing it if we don't have a guide."

At her words, I try not to think of Nico. I ultimately fail.

"Kappa might know the way out," Thomas suggests. Kappa is working downstairs since she doesn't need to take a break to eat, and they needed extra help since everyone is up here.

I nod. "Alright. Sounds good. I'll message you guys when I have enough information and we have a good slot to escape. Be ready for a MindSpeak thread sometime soon."

"Right," they say in unison.

I try to stop fidgeting throughout dinner and focus on the home cooked meal, knowing it could be my last for a while. After dinner, we make it back to our respective Long Rooms and pack our things as inconspicuously as possible.

Even so, I can't escape my brother's scrutiny.

"Jackie?"

I freeze, my heart plummeting.

Nicholas walks around me and plunks himself on the bottom bunk, in front of my bag.

"You're all leaving," he states rather than asks, his eyes downcast and filled to the brim with disappointment.

"I can't take you with me," I tell him.

I can't put him in danger again. Last time, he was captured by Evils and held hostage with the whole camp. I need to make sure he's safe, and the safest place I know is with the Indifferents and away from me.

Nico's shoulders slump. "Yeah, I get it. I'm useless."

I stare at him. "What? No! It's just— It's just too dangerous out there."

He smiles wanly, his eyes far too old and tired to belong to an eight-year-old. "Even my job is useless. No one needs my help anymore. But it's okay, Jackie."

"Nico—"

"I'll help you get out," he says. "Who's going with you? Thomas and Cali?"

I nod, speechless.

He slides off the bed.

"Light's out!" the Captain calls, as usual. He disappears out the door to wherever he retires for the night, before I get a chance to talk to him like I planned.

Nico doesn't say anything as we all climb into our bunks, not even bothering to note that I haven't changed into sleepwear. He just pulls his blanket over his head.

I lie awake, dread pooling in my stomach, until I hear the click of boots against the cold floor. They grow closer and stop outside our door. My eyes snap open, and I shift in my bunk carefully, squinting as I peer through the space between my mattress and the metal bars that keep me from falling out.

There's a tall figure at the door, its shape dark against the dim lighting of the hallway's safety lights. It flits away from the door. Before I can properly assess the situation, I'm out of my bunk and shaking Thomas awake.

# Chapter XII

## —Travis—

## **Important**

The streets are still empty, and the rest of the militia hasn't pursued us. Snow flits around, twirling through the air. I left the coat back at the fight, but we don't have time to retrieve it. For now, I just tug my sleeves over my knuckles and bear it. I hear a faint ringing in my ears. I ignore it at first, but as we walk along the side of the street, it seems to grow into an ongoing drone.

"Do you hear that?" I ask, hurrying to keep up with HG's brisk pace as I hold back curses, the soles of my feet stinging.

"Mm? You mean the chanting?"

"Chanting? No, like this hum—"

"Ah," she says. "Yes, the rally."

We halt for a second as HG looks around a corner, then continue our trek toward a large, immaculate building. Even from a distance, the architecture is impressive; it seems to shine among the bland townhouses that surround it. We're farther into the city now, and the buildings stretch higher into the sky the deeper we go.

"Every day at noon a rally is held," HG explains brusquely. "The citizens sing patriotic songs and recite laws, one of the Important makes a speech, and then everyone disperses to their normal activities. The rallies themselves are quite boring."

"So, the Light …" I deftly switch the topic to something more pressing, not caring about rallies I'll never go to. "You told me he's the leader of Kaltic."

"Yes," she says, jogging around a building before veering back on our main path.

"What's … he like?" I gasp out between breaths. She's a lot faster than me, and my lungs are working arduously to breathe in the icicles being shoved down my throat as I try to keep up with her.

HG doesn't so much as glance over her shoulder. Her voice drops. "He's colder than Kaltic."

She doesn't elaborate and I don't ask what she means. I lock down on the trek and push myself farther, despite my wound's protestations and the prickling chill that bites at my arms.

HG finally does look back and her eyes widen a fraction. "Are you sure you're okay?"

I nod vehemently and huff out a breath. "Map. Keep going. I'm right behind you."

She exhales and drops back beside me. "And once we get the map, you can figure things out, right?"

Snow crunches behind us. "Figure out what things?"

I whip around, my entire body screaming at the abrupt movement. My shoulders are squared, and I hold my arm up, ready to transform the stone into a weapon.

The young man who faces me is probably in his thirties, though he's a few inches shorter than me. His pale face is friendly, framed by short golden hair. The man grins at me, and all I can wonder is how he managed to sneak up on us. A side alley, perhaps? Was he following us the entire time, tracking our conversation?

I narrow my eyes, but HG bows her head. "Good day, Yield."

"Good day," he answers with a nod. "What are you doing?"

"Sir," HG says politely, though her green-gray eyes flash in irritation. "We were just on our way to the Light's office."

The man steps back, his hands folded in front of him. "I assumed so. Who is this with you, HG-8057? All civilians are supposed to be at the rally unless they are in the militia or have authorized permission to be absent. I also presumed you'd still be in questioning. Which reminds me, I heard there was an outsider in holding?"

I watch their interaction cautiously, hoping I look less conspicuous than I feel.

HG frowns. "I was let out with another warning."

When his smile widens, it rivals the radiance of the sun. "Good for you, HG-8057! I'm glad you're not in too much trouble. But I was asking you about your partner." He nods his head in my direction. "Who is this? It's awfully chilly out with just a shirt. Funny, you don't have a tag."

HG and I both open our mouths to answer.

"Here." He shoulders off his own coat, holding it out to me. "I'm not technically in a position to question you since you aren't a civilian. You're the outsider, I assume? I'm the Yield. It won't do for you to be outside without any proper clothing. Good luck with the Light, if he's in, that is." He glances at HG. "You know his schedule better than me, HG-8057. Anyway, outsider, hopefully you get enlisted as a member of Kaltic so I can officially scold you for not wearing appropriate outdoor attire. Have a great day!"

I blink, and the words I prepared vanish. HG seems at a loss as well. The Yield waves at us before he trots off in the direction of the chanting. Holding the coat he gave me at arm's length, I check all the pockets and seams for bugs or a tracking device, but it's just a regular old tan jacket with fluffy lining.

"Excuse me, but what was that?" I ask, reluctantly slipping the coat on. It isn't already warm as I assume it would be with the Yield wearing it.

"I'm not sure what he's playing at, but it doesn't matter," HG grumbles. "We should hurry. We don't want to get caught by the Axe."

HG takes the lead to the Capital building, the same ornate one I saw in the distance. It's even bigger up close, as if being the grandest thing in the whole urban area proclaims its importance. I glance around the streets warily, on edge and confused after our encounter with the Yield. How could he be so trusting with a couple of suspicious kids, especially seeing as I'm the "outsider"? As far as he knew, I was on my way to assassinate the Light with a mutinous accomplice. And yet, he greeted us, asked few questions, didn't get a straight answer, and gave me his coat so I wouldn't freeze.

HG thinks he's playing at something, and I agree. No one is kind or helpful for no reason. Not in this world. Though, Kaltic seems more and more like a whole new planet the longer I'm here.

We ascend the steps to the magnificent building. The double doors are huge, probably nine feet tall. HG pushes on the handle and lets us in. The lobby is just as impressive as the exterior, with gold chandeliers and patterned wallpaper. There's a vacant reception desk on the other side of the room.

"It's empty?" I ponder aloud.

"Yes. Everyone should be at the rally. It's not as if every day they get people sneaking in to rob the Capital, you know."

"Right," I mutter as HG heads for the stairs without hesitation, like she's done this a thousand times.

Each step gets heavier and heavier for me, and by the second flight, my legs tremble and my abdomen aches. I normally have a high pain tolerance and higher physical endurance, but fighting people and tromping around Kaltic with a stomach wound is taking its toll on me.

I'm surprised I lasted this long, considering the circumstances.

"Travis." HG looks back. "Are you—"

*"Fine,"* I hiss, still catching my breath. "I'm fine. Don't forget why we're here."

"Two more flights," she assures me, slowing for me to catch up, to my displeasure.

I grit my teeth and make an effort to hurry. I don't need her concern or sympathy, and I can't afford to slow down. My knuckles turn white as I grip the banister and force my numb feet to keep climbing. One step folds into twenty, and by then I've lost count.

We end up in a hallway. HG stops right outside a closed wooden door. A plaque on the wall beside it reads, *The Light*.

"You ready?" she asks me.

"This is the most important thing right now. I have to be."

"Alright. He should be back in about thirty minutes from a council meeting, so we need to be quick."

With that, she takes a deep breath, places her hand on the doorknob, and pushes the door open.

# Chapter XIII

## —Jack—

## Flight

Thomas and I silently creep to the door, our bags slung over our backs in case we have to make an impromptu getaway, only to be startled by Nico, who's crouched in the doorframe.

"What are you doing?" I hiss, my heart rate not exactly going down.

"Same as you." He shrugs, gesturing toward the hallway. "You saw him, right?"

We nod. Thomas's eyes are wide, while Nico just stares into the darkness with a tight expression on his face.

"You don't think it's another invasion, do you?" Thomas asks.

"No," Nico whispers. "It was Alistair. He's going in the direction of the hatch."

My breath catches. "We need to go after him."

Nico's emerald eyes are teal in the light of the stone, growing rounder as the realization dawns on him. "He's leaving?"

I exhale, stepping back inside the Long Room to grab our bags, just in case.

"We need to go after him," I repeat, sliding back into the hallway. "Now."

"What about Cali?" Thomas says.

My eyes meet Nico's, and he gives me a resolute nod. "I'll get her. Wait here. I'll take you guys to the hatch."

He sprints into the dark, and I'm about to call after him, tell him to get a light or take my stone at least, but he's gone.

"Let's hope the Captain isn't already gone," Thomas mutters as we wait with bated breath.

Nico's back in a few minutes, Cali in tow. Her hair is tangled from sleep, but otherwise she looks energetic and ready.

"How'd you get back so fast?" I ask, impressed yet mildly concerned. "It's so dark."

Nico waves for us to follow before looking over his shoulder at me. "My ability. I have the tunnels memorized. I just closed my eyes and ran."

Then he dashes ahead, and we scramble after him, taking sharp turns, finally stopping at the hatch room.

I leap onto the ladder and pull myself up and out of the hatch, ignoring the trapdoor's noisy clang against the roof when I slam it open.

"What the—" comes a voice, and then, "Barret?"

Rolling onto my knees, I push myself to my feet and face the Captain, who's staring at me like he's seen a ghost. Cali, Thomas, and Nico join me on the roof.

"What are you all doing out here?" the Captain growls.

"We were wondering the same about you," I say levelly. "You never told us you were leaving."

He clicks his tongue. "It's none of your concern."

I fold my arms. "I heard you're going south."

He stiffens. "Who told you that?"

"No one," I reply. "But south is where it's really cold, right? Colder than here. Colder than anywhere."

"Yes. What's it to you?"

"In the south, they have lots of snow, right?" I continue, trying to paint my dream for him. "And huge rock formations. There's tall steel buildings, y'know."

The pale moonlight catches his dark onyx eyes, and something akin to recognition glints in them. *Aha.*

"Have you been there?" I ask. "Where there's fields of snow and mountains on either side."

"How do you …" He falters. "What's your point?"

"We're looking for Travis, our friend," I say bluntly. "The only thing I know is that he's alive and he's connected to that place. I can't reach him personally, though."

"And you want me to take you there," he finishes. "Sorry, but that's not my problem. I already have a destination in mind."

An idea pops into my head, half-baked at best, but an idea, nonetheless. "We can help you. And you can help us. You know how to get to the south."

"Listen, Barret," he says, "it's nice of you to volunteer, but I don't need your help. It seems you need my expertise more than I need a handful of extra kids to babysit, so I'll have to politely decline."

I bite my lip, trying to come up with anything to get him to help us. He's right; we're more of a burden to him. But since he knows something about the only connection I have to Travis, we need his help.

Thomas steps forward, his normally warm eyes steely and calculating. "That's quite a shame, sir, seeing as we have a method of travel far more effective than getting around on foot."

The Captain's midnight eyes flick down to Thomas, and he grudgingly says, "Go on."

"We have Kappa," Thomas reminds him with a smile. "She was our mode of transportation before the battle, and she can easily keep up with speeds only horses can reach. Probably faster."

He whistles. "That *would* be helpful. So then, why do you want me? There are other people who know about the southern regions. Why go through the trouble of asking someone who is in the best position to report you for this?"

Thomas glances at me as if to say, *I set this up for you, but you have to finish the deal.*

I stare at my boots. "I can't reach the people that would be the most helpful. Besides, we know you well, and it wouldn't make sense to ask just anyone. You're also leaving, so we don't need to convince someone who doesn't really want to go. And you're not old."

He snorts. "Fair enough. Where's your robot?"

With a high-pitched whistle, Thomas calls Kappa out. Seconds later, she stands on the roof with her hand on her hip, her face somewhere between unimpressed and apathetic.

"We weren't going to leave you," Thomas promises her. "We just had to catch the Captain first, is all."

She smiles in that not-quite-human way of hers. "Yes, I see that."

At Thomas's command, she transforms into a hulking machine with wiry legs that crack against the concrete roof. Her bronze body glows silver under the moonlight, and in the dark, she appears more like a spider than anything. The Captain stands idly to the side as Cali lifts our bags onto Kappa with her ability, setting them near the back. Metal straps rise up to secure them.

I'm watching her load our stuff when a tap on my arm diverts my attention. Nicholas's hand drops, and he inhales slowly.

"Nico—"

"You better come back safe," he interrupts, his emerald eyes reflecting the moon and giving them a glassy look.

"I will. I promise. You'll need to take care of the camp for me, and because the Captain'll be gone too."

He nods, sniffing. "Yeah."

I place a hand on his shoulder. "Y'know, Nico, I dunno where you ever got the idea that you're useless. Tonight just proves otherwise. I'm … really proud of you."

"Jackie …"

"It's going to be just fine," I assure him, wrapping him in a hug. "We'll find Travis and come back."

"I know." He buries his face in my coat and hugs me back.

Finally, he lets go and steps back to the hatch.

"See you then," I say, moving toward Kappa.

"Mhm." He smiles then, and it's not sad. "I love you, Jackie."

"Love you too."

With that, he's gone. The hatch shuts firmly behind him. The others climb onto the robot, saying nothing.

Once we're all situated, I look down at the Captain, who hasn't climbed aboard yet. He eyes the robot skeptically, hints of hesitance clear on his face. He seemed to accept the idea at first, but now that Kappa is here and we're ready to go, he looks nervous.

"Are you scared?" Cali teases, prompting him to fold his arms and cast her a glare.

"Don't be ridiculous," he says before hauling himself aboard, albeit a little more slowly than the rest of us.

We all take a last look at the building, the Captain staring a bit longer.

"Goodbye," he tells the closed hatch.

The stone is warm against my wrist in the frigid midnight air. It reminds me of home and of family. After all, my home isn't in a building. It's with the people I love. And even though Nico isn't with us, I know he's not unreachable.

Unlike a certain missing someone.

*We're coming, Travis,* I think, wishing for the first time that my thoughts weren't trapped in my mind.

"What direction is south?" Thomas asks the Captain.

"At seven o'clock. It's a straight path to the city I'm aiming for," the Captain replies. "I plan on finding some old friends too. After that I'll hold up my end of the deal and take you where you want to go."

We nod. Thomas relays the directions to Kappa, and she turns around. Her metal legs creak as she crouches and then bolts off the roof.

And we're off, just us and the world.

# Chapter XIV

## —Travis—

## Recapture

The stench of coffee hits me like a brick wall to the face as the door opens. I flash back to when I first woke up in the cell with that bittersweet smell hanging softly in the air. Now it's strong enough to make me feel extremely nauseous, and I wonder if the smell itself is a defense mechanism. HG does not seem fazed, though.

We both step inside, and HG shuts the door, making my chances of tactical escape slimmer: I haven't eaten anything since I woke up in the cave, but my stomach churns as the overpowering odor hovers in the room like a cloud, engulfing us both. My mind is muddled, and half of me wants to fade back through the door and collapse against the wall. I know HG is moving forward already, hurrying across the dark polished wood floor to the desk near the back of the room.

I can barely reign my thoughts in, and it's at this moment that I officially swear off coffee. It's not that I hate it. Before I left the Evils, I couldn't seem to get enough of it. Coffee is scarce, and it's very expensive. So much so that my team had to steal it.

I can't stand it any longer. I choke out, "You have coffee here?"

HG pauses her search and turns around to look at me as if she just realized I'm not being helpful. "We grow a lot of it. Why?"

"You mean you don't— *God*, you don't smell that?"

She peers at me, her mouth set in a frown. "Pardon?"

"I— Ugh, never mind."

"Can you come over here?" she asks. "You'll have more of an idea of what you are looking for than I do."

"Right." I stumble over to the desk and catch myself on the edge. "Maybe you should watch the door."

She nods and I walk around the desk, scanning its many drawers. The surface is bare except for a notebook and a couple of pens. I crouch, still trying not to gag, and pull on one of the drawer handles. It's stuck.

I try all the drawers and find them all locked.

Cursing under my breath, I stand up shakily and survey the room. Bookshelves line the white walls, but aside from the velvet rug in the middle of the room and the shelves and desk, there's nothing here. The walls are mostly bare except for these metal rods that I assume are decorative.

"Travis?" HG calls. "I think someone's coming."

I hold my breath. The subtle thudding vibration through the wooden floorboards pounds in my head and chest. Gritting my teeth, I motion at HG to move to the wall. If the door opens, she'll be hidden temporarily.

After that we'll have to figure it out.

Dashing across the room, I stand next to HG behind the door, my shoulder barely an inch from hers. I switch the stone to a gun and hold it under my sleeve to conceal the glow. Glancing at HG, I find myself wishing I had Jack's ability, to communicate with her silently. I just hope she doesn't do anything stupid if we get caught.

The door creaks open, nearly brushing my nose. Sharp footsteps fill the dead air. They tap away, toward the desk, and stop abruptly.

And then the voice comes, weathered and gruff. "I know you're there, outsider."

I kick the door away and grab HG's shoulder, forcing her to take a step forward as I point the gun at her head.

"Play along," I whisper, though I can't tell if she heard me.

The man regards me coldly, his pale green eyes a mirror image of HG's. He holds himself with a certain confidence, and I assume he's the Light. I study him warily, noting how oddly similar he and HG look, from the sharp angles of their faces to their platinum-blond hair. A bold idea sparks in my mind.

"Now," I say, "she doesn't know what's going on, but you might."

"What are you talking about?" the Light asks. "And what are you doing in my study?"

I go for one of my crazy-Evil grins and try my luck. "Poor HG. Even after I forced her to take me all this way, and threaten her in front of her *father*, you still won't do anything. Just give me what I want, and I'll consider sparing both of you."

"What do you plan to do?" he asks, unimpressed. I note that he didn't deny HG is his daughter. "You're cornered. I suppose it is admirable that you've gotten this far. What have you come here to do? Kill me?"

"I'm not scared of you," I state, keeping my voice level. "But you should be scared of me."

"Scared? No. However, I do feel a bit sorry for you."

"You'll definitely be feeling sorry," I growl, the threat sliding easily off my tongue. "When I'm done with both of you."

The bookshelves on both sides of the room seem to close in on us, the blood-red drapes on the window leering from behind the leader of Kaltic. In this moment, it's just me glaring menacingly at the Light, whose calm yet furious expression sends a shiver down my spine. His face is neutral, reminding me of AR, but the tight line of his mouth and near his eyes, and the dark glint in his pupils betray rage.

His stare meets mine and my detached instincts don't notice something in him tense until it's too late. He grabs a metal stick that's pointed at both ends off a hook on the wall. With a click, the object comes flying toward us. I kick HG out of the way, and everything moves in slow motion as I watch the metal point at my heart.

I shut off my senses, my body shifting into full-force fading. I barely register the thing as it passes through my chest as if I'm not here. It sails through the coffee-bogged air and hits something on the wall behind me.

"The alarm!" HG gasps before my hearing cuts out.

Without my sight or hearing, all I can feel are the tremors in the floor as something pounds up the stairs. Then that's gone too, and I find myself suspended in oblivion as the coffee smell retreats into nothingness.

I grope numbly around what I assume is the floor, the stone the only thing I can feel. I wrap my fingers around it, using its unusual warmth as a lifeline.

I'm still in a faded state, though I can vaguely tell I haven't gone through the floor. My muscles are limp beneath me. Using only my knowledge of the situation before I lost all touch, I deduce that I'm kneeling on the floor near HG's feet.

Shadows and shapes flit around the emptiness, and my head seems to float, becoming lighter and lighter.

*I'm reaching my limit,* I realize belatedly. *I need to stop fading. I need to get up. I need to fight.*

The cord securing my head to my body snaps, and my coherent thought process diminishes to a steady throb. As I lose consciousness, my senses creep back in slowly.

The polished wood floor is cool beneath my heavy limbs. There's the stench of coffee, but I'm too tired to be bothered.

"—avis! Travis!" a girl's voice reaches me.

"He really thought he could take me on," says a gravelly voice. "But he is no match for the machines of Kaltic."

I process colors. The wail of sirens. Rough hands dragging me up. I grasp at whatever bits of wakefulness I can, but I'm slipping.

"Wait! Travis!"

I'm slipping away.

# Chapter XV

## —Jack—

## Family

We bound over buildings, and I pretend I don't see the Captain clutching the metal handles for dear life.

Once we get to the ground, the ride is smooth enough for everyone to calm down and hold a conversation without the possibility of biting our tongues off.

"Uh, Captain?" Thomas calls quietly.

The Captain holds a fist over his mouth for a second, looking greenish under the pale moonlight. "Don't … Don't call me Captain anymore. Just Alistair, or sir. If someone we don't know overhears you calling me that, we could get into big trouble, especially if that someone is an Evil team. Or a Good team, if I'm being honest."

"How come?" Cali asks.

"People will always jump to conclusions," Alistair says. "Captain is a high rank, and if someone thinks we're their enemy, we could be captured for ransom, for a team we don't belong to. Or, we could get called into service by someone who thinks we're on their side. Best to stick with plain names out here, where people can get less of a hold on you."

"Makes sense, I guess," I say. "So, Cap— I mean Alistair, you promise you're going to help us after we find your friends, right?"

"Sure, yes," he replies. "You said you're looking for a friend? This Travis person. If I recall correctly, he died the morning of the battle."

"He's not dead," I say indignantly. "I already said that."

"How do you know?"

"Nora said so, and … it's just a feeling," I mumble. "Besides, I had dreams. About the snowy place. And Nora said he told her he's trying to sort out an issue, so he must have made it somewhere. I'd ask him myself, but it's odd, y'see. I can't reach him. It's like he's totally blocked off."

Alistair's eyes narrow. "I see."

We fall into an awkward silence after that, as the gray and dilapidated buildings whip by.

Kappa continues to charge ahead, zooming through streets and over decrepit brick structures. We spike up the buildings and vault over the rooftops, heading for the southern wall. Kappa hurtles toward it, and I hold my breath as we run vertically up the wall and over it. I smile in spite of myself at Cali's whoops and Alistair's halted screaming.

"Kappa, stop!" Thomas commands, once we're a good distance from the city.

The abrupt motion throws me forward, and I sit up, wiping my bangs out of my eyes. "Why'd we stop?"

Thomas points at Alistair, who promptly throws up over the side of the robot.

He grabs his own canteen of water, takes a swig, and wipes his mouth. "Fine. Keep going."

"It's still dark, though," Cali notes. "We should probably stop for the rest of the night."

I look up at the full moon between the clouds. The air is slightly warmer than in the city, but it's still quite cold.

"She's right," Thomas agrees. "I don't like the idea of traveling so much in the dark. We should rest, especially since we'll have to keep moving for a while."

Alistair nods hesitantly, though he looks relieved. "Good call."

We slide off Kappa and huddle under her tall figure, using a lantern Alistair brought to set up a temporary camp. Cali rummages around our packs for blankets while Alistair takes some bread from a bag and hands it around.

We sit on our blankets in a semi-circle around the flickering lantern and nibble at our bread rations.

"Hey, Alistair," Cali says quietly. "Can you tell us about these friends we're going to meet?"

"Sure," he says, leaning against one of Kappa's legs. "Let me think. Well, before I joined up with the camp, I ran around with a group of kids my age who grew up with me in a small village away from the Goods and Evils. Actually, they were the ones who originally gave me my nickname, and one of my friends who followed me into the camp carried it over. But the ones we're looking for now are people I consider family."

"How come they didn't join the camp with you and your other friend?" Thomas asks, settling on his side.

"They didn't trust your kind of society. You know, with jobs and curfew and moving every decade or so. I felt safer in a big group, and they were more comfortable by themselves."

"What are their names?"

"Miriam, Ezra, and Tova," Alistair says wistfully. "Miriam was like my little sister, and Ezra was like a brother. He was my best friend. Tova always acted like our mother, even though she was our age, and if you asked them, they'd probably tell you I seemed like a father." He pauses. "Is that weird?"

"No," I answer. "Reminds me of my friends."

"You're right." Thomas grins, his face illuminated by the lantern's light. "Travis and Nora and you and me and Cali. But now Alistair is part of our family."

I chuckle. "Yeah. He's like our grandpa."

Alistair scoffs.

Cali giggles.

*What about my real family?* The thought stabs at my mind. *What about Nico and my parents?*

I falter, feeling a bit more morose. We sit in silence.

"You all should sleep," Alistair says finally. "I'll keep watch … with Kappa."

Thomas stretches and nods. Cali's already asleep, bundled in her blanket. I yawn, pulling my own blanket over my shoulders.

I sense Alistair get up and walk around, muttering things to himself. My own sleep is short. I try to contact Nora and Cole, to no avail. I decide against visiting my parents, as they don't need to know I'm gone, as long as I come back.

And I will come back.

When I open my eyes again, Alistair is still sitting outside of the shelter of Kappa. It's almost dawn, and the black sky is fading to a dull indigo. I get up and sit next to him, thinking about my family. My families.

Gazing at his tired face out of the corner of my eye, I wonder if someone can belong to multiple families and still be completely alone.

***

We finish off the leftovers of last night's bread for breakfast as the sun comes up. We're all quiet for the most part, not really having anything to talk about other than some plans from Alistair for when we start moving again.

We all get ready to head out, folding our blankets and repacking. Alistair says the city we're going to is not too far from here. It's the same one our camp passed through when he joined them. I was a toddler at the time, so I can't remember any of it.

He warns us about rogue groups and that we need to be careful once we enter the city, not just because of human threats, but because of the odd condition of the city. He doesn't elaborate, though.

We climb back on Kappa and bound through the dry wasteland, passing dead trees and bushes, and pounding through the sparse brown grass. As the hours tick by without any sign of danger except for the heat that attempts to cook me alive, we play mind games to pass time.

"Would you rather eat a shoe or bathe in sawdust?" Cali asks.

"Uh … bathe in sawdust? Why would anyone try to eat a shoe?" I say.

She shrugs. "I dunno. Who's next?"

Alistair raises his right hand and points at a rusted yellow blob on the horizon. "You can see the city now."

We crane our necks and squint at the distant city.

"Why's it like that?" Cali asks.

"Hm?"

"Why's it yellow?" she clarifies.

Alistair's expression darkens. "To put it simply, it's polluted. There's a lot of radiation and dust floating around in there. 'Radiation station,' that's what people call cities or areas that are nearly too toxic to live in. Not exactly a dead zone, though. I don't think you'll fare too badly, being born in radiation, but let's try to be careful."

"What do you mean?" I ask.

"The air is bad," Thomas simplifies, his eyes narrowed at the horizon. "Cap— Alistair, just how bad is it?"

"It'll most likely be hard to breathe in there," he says. "And the atmosphere may burn a little, but I haven't been there in a long time, so I can't say for certain. I just hope they've survived."

Alistair's grim expression doesn't invite any more questions or conversation. I rub the stone thoughtfully, wondering how bad this city could be, and how the air could burn. The stone sends a shock up my arm as if in response, but it doesn't feel comforting. It's a warning.

We move quickly over the rough terrain, soon growing closer to a peculiar cluster of shapes. As we get nearer, I find that they're tents, along with crates stacked around what looks like a makeshift camp.

Alistair sees it too and his shoulders tense in apprehension as his gaze focuses.

I don't notice any people, but the place doesn't feel deserted either. Smoke rises from one of the tents, and clothes hang on a line near it.

"Alistair?" Cali asks. "Are those your friends?"

"No," he mutters. "We should go far around—"

*Clank! Clank!*

An alarm that sounds like metal pots banging together rises from the camp. A hoard of people comes running from the tents, and the once-silent ghost-camp roars to life.

Alistair curses under his breath at the sight of the rough-looking people, all wearing shades of black and red.

"Do you know them?" I whisper.

"Look at their clothes," Alistair hisses back. "Evils."

"Stop!" a tall man in a leather jacket booms.

At once, all the Evils raise their weapons. Even if we tried to bolt past them, they could easily open fire on us. Thomas seems to understand this too, and he tells Kappa to halt.

I shove my hands in my pockets, hiding the stone.

"What do we do?" Cali mumbles.

"We try to negotiate passage. There's a chance they'll leave us alone," Alistair answers quietly. "And there's a chance they won't. Don't worry, I'll take care of it."

"Oi," the tall man calls. "That robot you got. It looks like one of ours. You on the recon team?"

Alistair peers at them. "We were sent to pick up the robot. Found it in the city next over. Our map got soaked and this idiot here"—he knocks me on the head—"lost the compass. Are we heading in the right direction?"

The man scowls. "Where you supposed to be takin' it?"

"To the nearest base," Alistair says.

"There's no bases out here for miles." The man narrows his eyes. "Y'all just a buncha kids. Why'd they send children on a mission like that? No wonder you got screwed over."

"We still have supplies, and the robot can take us around," Alistair says.

"A'ight, but you can join our team until the band picks us up. They'll be here soon."

Alistair stiffens. "No, we're doing fine. We don't need your help, thanks."

The man shrugs. "It ain't pretty around here. That city back there's pretty dead. You might as well stay with us. Word came in just a day ago that our teams are closing in on this area from the north, west, and east, and soon. If you wanna make it to your team or back to claimed territory, waiting here's your best bet. There ain't nowhere else to go."

"I told you, we're fine." Alistair's voice is steady, but his eyes are narrowed, thoughtful.

A girl in a black trench coat dashes up to the man and whispers something to him, and his suspicious glare hardens.

The man is silent for a beat, then says. "I see. You think I'm stupid?"

Alistair doesn't back down from his original lie. "Of course not. We just have an agenda."

The man holds up his hand and all the weapons train on us again, clicking for emphasis. "I know y'all aren't with the organization."

Thomas's brown eyes are wide, and he turns back to Alistair. "Captain!"

"Thomas—" Alistair's calm mask creeps toward panic.

"Captain?" the tall man repeats. "*Oh*, y'all are Goods, aren't you?"

A dawning realization crosses Alistair's face, a connection between only him and Thomas sparking in the tense air.

"You don't understand," Alistair says, addressing the man. "I'm a Captain in our organization. This robot takes orders from me."

The Evils lower their weapons a bit. Thomas exhales a sigh of relief through his nose, though his hand is white against Kappa's surface.

"Kappa, walk left," Alistair directs as if to prove it.

Thomas taps on Kappa and she complies. The panic subsides, and for a moment I'm convinced we have this all under control.

"Where's your badge?" the man asks then.

"I—"

"Fire!" the man roars. "Take down the robot too. It's gone rogue."

The Evils train their firearms on us, and those without guns raise their knives menacingly.

Alistair stands up, muttering under his breath, and a breeze shakes his coat despite the calm, windless air. A thousand shots sound at the same time Alistair leaps, and the earth rumbles. We go flying backward as the ground jumps and cracks and a wind gushes at us.

The Evils shout in surprise, and I wonder what happened and where the bullets went, since none of us seem to be harmed, Kappa included. I crouch behind Kappa, who's mostly shielding us now, and peek out slowly from behind her large metal figure.

All I can see is dust blanketing my line of sight with its foggy particles.

"What happened?" Cali coughs.

"I don't know," I answer. "Is everyone alright?"

"Yeah," Thomas says, his back pressed against Kappa. "Can you see what's going on out there? I can't hear any more shooting."

He's right. The only sounds are deafening, gritty crashes and the low grumbling of the earth.

We wait until Alistair comes jogging back to us, his face pale and his frame trembling.

"What did you do?" I ask.

"Get on the robot," is his only reply.

We hastily climb back onto Kappa. Under Thomas's command, she bounds through the smoke and dust toward the city. As we grow closer, I notice the tinted sky and a sickly cloud that hangs over the city like a smog. The air tastes stale and sour, and there are considerably fewer shrubs and plants the farther we go.

Soon, the city walls are looming over us, casting grim shadows over the ground. We enter the cracked gates and stroll right into radiation station.

# Chapter XVI

## —Travis—

## The Mind

*The machines of Kaltic.*

HG's mention of them repeats like a mantra in my head. I'm staring blankly at the surface of a desk. The alarms …

We really screwed up.

I blink, looking around. I'm in a small room, seated in an uncomfortable metal chair. Across the table, a lean man with cocoa-colored skin, short black hair, and startlingly sharp crystal-blue eyes stares at me. Welding goggles rest on his forehead, and his gloved hands are folded over the desk.

Deciding not to speak, I breathe in deeply and let my gaze flick around the room, considering the only exit. He's positioned in front of me in a way that blocks the door; he could easily intercept me if I tried to get past. With how exhausted I feel, I doubt there'd be much of a fight.

"You seem alert," the man notes. "Can you hear me?"

I slowly meet his eyes. Cooperating seems like the best choice, since I don't know where I am, and we're alone. I briefly wonder where HG is.

"Yes," I mutter.

"I am the Mind," he says. "I was told your title is Travis."

I don't answer.

"I was allowed to oversee you, as you prove to be an interesting case." His eyes bore into mine, as if he sees not just me, but beyond.

"So you don't plan to kill me?" I reiterate.

"Well, I'd assume not. After my experiments, I'm not sure what your fate will be, but if all goes well, you'll probably be transferred to the Yield."

"You're going to experiment on me?"

"Yes. I was informed that you have special abilities. From the reports, these abilities come with limits. Care to give me some insight? I assure you all information is confidential, and you do not need to go into detail. You may also ask me questions. But the more you tell me, the easier this will be. Your choice."

"And if I decide not to talk?"

He smiles. "There are multiple ways of getting information out of someone."

That's a threat I'm used to: used to hearing, used to saying. He contains his emotions behind a wall, all his words calculated. Even under the guise of having a "choice," I don't have room to choose. He mentioned that I might be transferred to the Yield if I cooperate, and it's because of this I decide. The Mind is dangerous; the sooner I leave, the better.

Whether or not I tell him everything about my ability, I assume he'll try to figure it out anyway. His proposition is intriguing, and I do need answers. But it's a trade. However, I'm betting on my ability to lie. Because when it comes down to it, the Mind isn't the only thing that's dangerous. All of Kaltic is. I'm not sure how crucial my information is, but if they were to enter the war or turn their attention to Jack and the stone, seeing as mine will definitely produce questions, then a lot of people would be in for a great deal of trouble.

I have to withhold as much information as I can without raising suspicion.

"Whatever your reports say, they're mostly right," I say, testing the extent of his knowledge first. "It strains my senses when I use my ability, and I often experience a lag or blackout if I'm exhausted."

He nods. "That would make sense, as you are most likely incinerating some nerves in the process of … What do you call it? Quantum tunneling? Transposing?"

"Fading. But what you said works."

His eyes light up. "How fascinating. I've always been interested in the idea of having solid objects pass through other objects seamlessly. All my attempts end up in evaporating my subjects, items of course. We should run tests, Travis. Find out how it works. Why you can do it.

"You see, something like that should not be physically possible, and it's especially hard to believe you can control such an ability through sheer will. So, you were born with it then? It wasn't something you acquired later on in life?"

"I was born with it," I confirm. "In the outside world, many people are born with abilities."

"In regards to the war, where were you born? How much do you know about abilities?"

So he knows about the war. His questions are straightforward and blunt, telling me two things: Kaltic isn't completely detached from the rest of the world, and he knows more than he lets on.

"I don't know where I was born, since I grew up on the road. I don't know much about abilities either, just that a lot of people have them." I switch the subject around. "May I ask you a few questions now?"

Short annoyance flickers across his face before he nods. "Yes, of course. Go ahead."

"How does the system of Kaltic work? How do you run this society?" I'm probing for information since he's so talkative. "Also, what is your policy on people like me?"

The Mind sits forward, resting his elbow on the table, his head on his hand. "The properties of Kaltic are separated into four quadrants that are ruled by the Light, the Axe, the Yield, the Judge, and me."

"Right," I say, mentally cataloging this.

He laces his fingers together over the table. "The Axe takes over the militia as well as threats, the Yield governs the civilians, the Judge is involved with law and order, and I'm Kaltic's engineer. We each run our departments accordingly and report to the Light. There is one other Important who does not have a branch—the Secretary, and she holds all of Kaltic's keys and schedules. Together, we make sure Kaltic stays as pure and pristine as possible. We've been doing it for decades."

"But you look pretty young," I point out, pretending not to notice that he hasn't answered my last question. "How long have you had your position?"

"Eighty-five years," he says with a short chuckle. "Perhaps my appearance deceives my age. The first Mind found a way to transfer the consciousness of a human being into an artificial body—a machine. All of the Important, the people with titles like me, we are part of the machines of Kaltic. Our titles get passed down, and once it is time for our predecessors to retire, we swap. They get our old bodies and die, while we live for a long time, until it is our turn. Only the most pure and specially trained can do this. Our machine bodies also retain the memories of the generations before us, so we have access to all knowledge in Kaltic regarding our special divisions.

"Think of it like reincarnation, almost."

"But how is that possible?" I ask, my eyes narrowed. "Swapping souls?"

His lips stretch into a thin smile. "Perhaps we will discuss that sometime, but right now, you must be rested for our experiments. I did enjoy speaking with you, though. I hope we can maintain this level of casualness."

His last sentence throws me off. There's nothing casual here, from the way I'm being restrained to his dodged answer. He never did explain what they do to outsiders, which sets me on edge. I suspect he's either keeping that from me or lying about it for a reason. A reason I won't like.

Though, he did let me in on information I otherwise would have thought secret.

*The machines of Kaltic,* I think. *What an interesting concept.*

With this technology, would it be possible for everyone to live forever?

# Chapter XVII

## —Jack—

## **Captain**

I remember one time we got a shipment of peppers from a traveling camp. To us they were exotic, and no one warned us about their spiciness. I took a huge bite out of one of them and cried. To this day, I can still feel the tingle on my tongue and throat.

Breathing the air in the city is like inhaling peppers. My lungs burn, and my sinuses and throat feel like I've poured boiling water through my nose. Cali and Thomas both choke and scramble for their water canteens.

"Don't," Alistair warns, his voice quiet and hoarse. "It's not going to help. You'll get used to it."

I fight the urge to scrub at my watering eyes. Kappa seems unaffected, but the closer we get to the city's center, the more I notice the rusted buildings and corroded metal poles.

"I nearly forgot the feeling," Alistair whispers.

We're too busy trying not to suffocate to answer.

Kappa forges ahead, often stopping to leap over or walk around holes in the road or crumbled buildings that have flooded into the streets.

"Just a little longer," Alistair assures us. By then, my eyes aren't watering so badly.

My skin itches under my coat. I ignore it and concentrate on my surroundings instead. The city is smaller than ours, and the buildings aren't quite as big or as tall. We arrive in an area with short buildings, each with its own paved path to the door. Withered grass struggles to survive in front of every structure.

Alistair calls this place "suburbia" and explains that separate families lived in each of the buildings, or houses. He says this way of living is still practiced in big cities and neighborhoods and ports, but it's more crowded.

"Here," Alistair says, wiping at his eyes. We stop in front of a brick house. "This is where I saw them last."

"We just wait, then?" Cali asks, her voice rough.

Alistair's eyes are downcast. "If they're here, they'll come out."

"Would you like me to knock?" I offer.

He shakes his head and slides off Kappa. "Good idea, but I'll go."

I watch him tread up the narrow, paved path to the front door, rap his knuckles against it once, then twice. There isn't an answer. The windows are boarded with ashen planks. From the outside, it appears abandoned.

Alistair walks back with a shrug and climbs up on Kappa again.

We do end up drinking water. Despite Alistair's apprehension, it feels somewhat better.

"The air is sharp," Cali says. "Like freezer air, but the opposite."

"Sure, that's one way to put it," Alistair murmurs.

"Toxic," Thomas adds. "Will it hurt us after long enough exposure?"

Alistair stares straight ahead. "Let's hope not."

"Do you think …" I start a thought, but I don't want to upset Alistair.

But how could anyone live for more than a week in these conditions?

"Just wait," he says.

We do wait, for maybe an hour or two. I lose track of time, not that I have anything to go by with the sun blocked by the murky sky. The longer we sit, the more bearable and less painful it is to breathe, though my face feels too warm and tingly. I end up getting off Kappa to stretch. I walk around the lawns of the houses, and peek in windows that haven't been covered up.

The insides of the houses are interesting. I'm familiar with furniture, of course, but it never occurred to me that people would use it for decoration or leisure. Unless there is a reason for a table in the middle of the sofas, other than to trip over. There are variations in the way the houses are decorated and personalized. It makes me wonder about the people who used to live here and what exactly happened to them. If they left before the radiation or eventually died in it.

"In terms of recycling, what do you want to do for this week?" A voice reaches me from down the sidewalk.

"I'm thinking we can finish the ice cream and save the containers for— *What in the world is that?*"

Alistair hops off Kappa. His boots hit the asphalt with a *smack*. I sprint back to Thomas and Cali, who were drawing in the dust that cakes the street. We all stand, wary of the people approaching. Kappa transforms back to a girl.

The voices belong to two figures, heavily dressed head to toe in an assortment of clothing. The taller of the two has a brown leather jacket, ripped black pants made of a material I don't recognize, and welding goggles. The other has a ragged coat that drops to her knees, ankle-high black leather boots, and a bandana across her nose and mouth. Her blond hair is tied up in a messy bun.

Alistair takes a few steps forward, swiping loose strands of hair away from his face. The two people edge toward us carefully.

"Alis…?" the lady trails off, her hazel eyes wide.

The other person breaks into a dead run and tackles Alistair, pinning his arms to his sides and sweeping him up in a bear hug. "Captain!"

His voice is raspy but distinctively male, his laughs short and winded. The woman walks up to us much more slowly, her eyes cold and serious.

After a minute, the man steps back and tugs off his goggles, revealing bright green eyes. He wipes his face with his sleeve, smearing grime on his cheek in the process. Despite the dust and grit, his face shines when he smiles. The woman slides her bandana off her face and lets it rest on her collar. Her lips are set in a frown as she strides over to Alistair, looking him over.

Thomas, Cali, and I watch their reunion awkwardly from beside Kappa.

"Tova, Ezra—" Alistair begins.

The woman, Tova, slaps him hard across the face. The rest of us flinch and move to aid him, but he holds out a hand to stop us.

"What are you doing here, Alistair?" Tova demands.

"Nice to see you again, too," Alistair mutters.

The second stranger, Ezra, puts a gloved hand on Tova's shoulder. "Calm down. He's back, isn't that enough for you?"

Tova narrows her eyes. "You look exhausted."

"Let him talk, woman," Ezra chides exasperatedly.

Alistair blinks. "You both sure have grown. What have you been up to for the past decade?"

"It's been that long?" Ezra smooths back strands of wavy black hair.

"About."

"Well, we've been doing trade," Ezra murmurs.

"What he means is that we've barely been scraping by," Tova snaps, a bitterness laced between her words.

Ezra takes a shuddering breath. "Wow, we really missed you."

Alistair smiles. "Judging from Tova's murderous glare, I can only assume so."

"I can't believe you remember where we live," Tova says with a sigh. "Well, we should head inside. Who are the kids with you?"

"Friends." Alistair nods to us. "They tagged along."

"And you brought them to this dump?" Tova exclaims. "You're an idiot. They'll end up like Miriam if they stay here for long."

"Hey—" Ezra warns.

"Miriam?" Alistair interrupts, his smile fading. "Wait, where is she? Why isn't she with you? Is she sick?"

"She's dead," Tova states flatly.

Alistair's expression hardens. "What happened to her?"

"We can talk more inside," Ezra says. "Come on."

We follow the pair up the sidewalk silently. The mood has plummeted from elation to a hanging sense of dread.

"You have a robot?" Tova comments as she unlocks the door to the house.

"Her name is Kappa," Thomas says.

Tova glances back at him. "Right."

Ezra ushers everybody in and locks the door. Cool, refreshing air smacks us: it feels less toxic, and I realize how bad it is out there, compared to the instant relief of the house.

"Air conditioning?" Alistair whistles. "Nice."

Ezra smiles sheepishly. "We traded it for every mirror in a five-mile radius, which is a *lot* of mirrors."

I walk farther into the main room, exploring without really snooping around. On the first floor in a semi-circle are various pieces of furniture—a mattress, a couple of chairs, and a table. To the side is a kitchen, and behind a separate door I can make out a bathroom. It looks so domestic and normal to me, resembling the little apartments I've seen in the Adults' Quarters back at camp, that I'm almost nostalgic.

"Sit wherever," Tova tells us, slipping off her coat and boots at the door and hanging extra pieces of clothing on a hook on the wall.

Ezra does the same, then he goes to the kitchen and starts preparing something.

I crash in one of the chairs, Alistair sits heavily in the other, and Thomas and Cali perch on the mattress. Kappa stands.

Ezra comes back with bowls of white, soft-looking food. He hands us spoons. The food looks like it's steaming, but the bowl is cold to the touch. I poke mine experimentally and the spoon dips into it, some of it melting around the utensil.

"What is this?" Cali asks.

Ezra grins. "It's called ice cream. A vendor came through a few weeks ago offering it for some condensed milk packets. It's one of the best things in the world. Try it."

I scoop some of the cold food into my mouth. It's cool and sweet; a flavor I can't quite recognize. It melts on my tongue like a soft and delicious ice cube, tasting somewhat of cheese, but better.

I shovel more and more of it into my mouth until it's all gone.

"This … is really good," Thomas says, licking his lips.

Cali hums in agreement, devouring another spoonful. I see Alistair has barely touched his ice cream, and I wonder if he somehow doesn't like it.

"Tell me what happened to Miriam," he says quietly.

Ezra's face screws up into a pained expression, and Tova leans against the wall, her brows furrowed.

"Her body couldn't take the pollution," Tova finally says. "She started coughing more than usual one day, complaining that her throat burned. Then a week later, she woke up saying she couldn't breathe. She had some pretty bad burns all over her body, but then again, we all developed them. A month after that incident she just … didn't wake up. She went out a lot more than we did before we thought about ways to prevent inhaling the dust and smoke. We learned," she says quietly and clears her throat. "We learned from that."

Alistair covers his mouth like he's going to be sick, and Ezra takes the ice cream from him, setting it back in the kitchen.

Tova shakes her head. "It's not just the exterior radiation burns and breathing in the dust. The air is too caustic. It's like inhaling acid. Even if you survive the stomach ulcers and radiation poisoning, it'll take out your lungs anyway. The slow burns you develop from the air don't help. So, we couldn't really have done anything when death is inevitable here—"

"And you tell me *I'm* the idiot?" Alistair shouts suddenly. "Why haven't you left? If you knew this city was killing you and you had a better chance out in the wilderness, why didn't you go? Why didn't you take her there after the first sign?"

"She wasn't fit for travel!" Tova's fists shake. "We'd all have died out there, starving and dehydrated."

"You know that's not a valid reason," Alistair growls. "You could have carried her, built a wagon with all the parts lying loose around here. You have time to trade a ton of mirrors for air conditioning, but you can't haggle your way out of here?"

"Fine!" Tova hisses. "Yeah, I regret not leaving ten years ago, I do. But you want to know the real reason we didn't go? We were too scared to leave after you left. The Evils patrol around the area outside all the time, and we're powerless against them without you. We hid because we don't know how to do anything else. We were waiting for you, Captain."

The rage evaporates, leaving Alistair's expression empty and defeated. He rests his head in his hands, his shoulders trembling.

"Well … Here I am," he whispers, his voice catching. "I'm here now."

# Chapter XVIII

## —Travis—

## **Through a Closed Door**

Rather than shipping me back to a cell, the Mind sets me up in his spare bedroom for the time being. No one seems concerned about the ruckus I created, making me wonder if they underestimate me or if they're fully confident in their ability to stop me from causing more trouble. Despite the Mind's lenient attitude, I assume he's laid-back for a reason.

I have odd dreams where I feel like someone is calling out to me. There's a connection, or a tug, but every time I pinpoint it, it's severed, cutting me off and leaving me stranded. I go through a rush of colors: scarlet, a bright aqua, and then a deep indigo. There are no thoughts or any intelligible processes to them, just phases that pass me by.

I wake up starving.

I'm tucked neatly into a thin yet cushy bed. The walls are white, and the floor is carpeted with many decorative rugs that overlap each other. I'm still wearing my clothes from before—coat, boots, and all—except the bandages around my torso have been changed. I vaguely remember the Mind helping me with that after the interrogation. The wound just feels numb, partly from the medicine he used, and partly from my still tingling senses. While there, they feel somewhat detached.

Even though it doesn't hurt, I don't believe in miracles, and I know this kind of wound will take weeks, maybe months, to heal.

I slide out from under the covers, and my boots land softly on one of the rugs. Standing up straight, I slip out of the room and into the narrow hallway. I make my way to the main room, which is attached to a kitchen and a cozy sitting place. My footsteps tap along the dark, shiny hardwood floor. I'm not trying to sneak up on anybody. Not this time, anyway.

The Mind sits on the sofa, flipping through books at extreme speeds then picking up new ones. He hears me approach, sets down the book he's holding, and turns to greet me.

"Good afternoon," he says politely. "I take it you may be hungry. Go ahead and sit at the table, and I'll prepare you something."

I remain standing and watch him walk to the kitchen. He pulls out a pot and sets it on the stove, then pours a cup of water and a packet of something into it. Sudden flashes of *déjà vu* make me lightheaded. Everything he does seems familiar, yet I've never experienced any of it before. Even on the Good team, no one cooked for me personally.

Against my wrist, the stone warms, though I'm not sure why.

The Mind mixes the pot's contents, setting timers periodically. It doesn't take long, and a few minutes later he turns around with a bowl of steaming orange soup. Or what looks like soup.

"Please do sit," he says. It's not a request.

I choose a chair at the table and he places the bowl in front of me. It smells good, but I've learned not to trust everything easily set before me.

"It's not poisoned," he adds, his eyes glinting knowingly. "I can see why an outsider would be hesitant, when the world out there is so"—he pauses, as if searching for the right words—"full of liars."

I pretend not to notice the way he emphasizes that last part. Instead, I pick up the spoon and stare at him pointedly. "You have experience out there?"

"How do you believe Kaltic was started? We came from somewhere." He gestures to the soup. "Eat. I would never poison my own test subject."

"Thanks." It comes out slightly sarcastic, but he doesn't say anything.

I sip the somewhat creamy liquid, finding its tangy flavor and combined warmth pleasant. The Mind watches me eat, which cancels out the good feeling.

He chuckles.

"What is it?" I ask, my spoon stopping midway.

"You have the Yield's coat," he explains.

"Oh, yeah. We ran into him and he just … gave it to me."

"That does sound like something the Yield would do." The Mind smiles. "He's always been quite generous. I do believe that is his favorite coat, and he gave it to an impure outsider. I'm fond of his kindness; it's very amusing."

I don't respond to his comment. The way he speaks reminds me of a computer or a robot, even when he states opinions. I'm not surprised by that; he said there is a human soul in that body.

Once I'm finished eating, the Mind jumps to his feet with a new enthusiasm. He motions for me to follow him, saying we will start conducting experiments and recording data now. Glancing at the walls, I try to conjure some quick plan to dash out of here while I'm able to, but there's nothing of use. I assume the front door is locked, and using my ability would exhaust energy I'd need to run. And I don't exactly know my way around, anyway. Deciding I don't have much of a choice, my only hope is to stay in one piece. My mind is blank, not wanting to dwell on the possible horrors that await me as I willingly walk to what could be my demise.

We descend into a basement and step into a lab with several metal tables, a desk covered in papers in the corner, bookshelves lining the left wall, and all sorts of hulking machines that sit along the other walls. There are small trinkets along with charts and models on the tables. The mess is overwhelming, though it *is* impressive.

"Welcome to my workroom," the Mind says. "Only a select few people ever get to witness it."

I hum in acknowledgment, wondering how long I am guaranteed to live under these experiments and if there's any way out of this at the last second.

"Now, to start, I need you to tell me absolutely everything about your life, especially events you've had with your ability," he says.

I narrow my eyes. We already had that short interrogation, and then, I didn't say much. I'm not sure why he expects me to share personal things when I barely gave him an answer for the most basic questions.

He pulls out a nearby chair and perches on the edge, pen and notebook in his hands. After waiting a moment with nothing from me, he looks up and frowns.

"What's wrong?" he asks. "I only ask this to get an idea of how you use your ability and the way it functions. You don't need to tell me your life story. I realize I said *everything*, but I meant everything of importance to me, so I have a basis on what you're doing when your ability is in use."

I clench my fists, debating how much I want to tell him. He left that decision to me, after all, and so far, I've taken advantage of it, but I don't know when that will wear out.

"My ability isn't really a complex thought process," I begin, choosing my words carefully. "It's sort of like an impulse I can switch on and off."

When he realizes I've stopped talking, he looks up again. "Is that it? I'm disappointed, Travis. I thought you might tell me more. I'm afraid I'll have to spell it out for you."

I raise an eyebrow. "Oh?"

"Your cooperation is not a choice." His voice drops away from its friendly demeanor. "Your two choices now are either to follow my instructions, or execution. It's generous of me to let you choose, Travis, because most touched wouldn't get this far under our system."

He stands, his shadow falling over me. I try not to react, but my body steps back anyway.

"With that being said, what will it be, Travis?" He smiles, though there's something cruel in the way he does it.

I swallow nervously, feeling the first drips of true fear snake their way down my spine. In here, I'm powerless. I can try to fight back, but my mind has already worked through all those scenarios, and no matter which moves I come up with, I always lose in the end.

I don't have any other choice.

"Fine," I grumble, taking another involuntary step backward.

He nods. "Good. Now, is there anything you've failed to mention in regards to your ability?"

I take a deep breath and try to relax. "Hm … Well, I already told you I don't know where I was born. As for experience, I'm used to my ability enough to not worry about physical threats."

The Mind jumps up and swings at my head with his chair. I shift into fading so fast, I'm barely able to register it, acting on instinct alone. The legs of the chair pass seamlessly through my head and neck, and he stumbles with the momentum. If I had been solid, he would have knocked me out.

He immediately sets the chair down again and starts writing notes, then he glances at me. "You can put the knife away; I'm not going to do that again."

It takes me a second to realize the stone has transformed into a dagger in my hand.

"Thank you, Travis," he says, walking to one of the machines by the wall. "You did exactly what I wanted to see. Come over here now."

I edge over to him and stand a few feet away so he can't take me by surprise like that again, no matter what he says.

"Speaking of the knife," he begins while working on a panel on the machine, "can you explain to me what exactly that glowing device you have is?"

"I don't know what it is," I lie. "It's just a tool."

"Do you know the extent of its capabilities at least?"

"It turns into weapons."

He focuses on me. "Is that it?"

"Yes." While I don't actually know much about the stone, I know enough that if the Mind were to find out, the safety of my friends and I could be compromised. "It was on me when I woke up outside of Kaltic."

"Speaking of which." The Mind rubs his stubbly chin. "How did you end up outside of Kaltic? We are surrounded by snow and mountains. According to HG-8057's account, she found you lying in the middle of a snowfield."

I exhale. "I don't know. Before I got here, I was in this battle and I got shot." I gesture to myself for emphasis. "And the next thing I knew, I woke up in a cave."

"How odd." He peers at me, tapping his leg with his pen. "Have you ever blacked out due to injury before and ended up somewhere else completely unaware?"

"No."

"Have you been shot before? How bad was this wound at the time of impact? And from then to now, how much do you think it has healed?"

Frowning, I answer these questions truthfully. "I have been shot, but never with a gun like that … Uh, I don't really know. All I remember during the battle was that it hurt worse than anything I've been through before, and I really thought I was dying. That I was dead. One of your medical staff stitched me up—when I first got here, I assume—and it bleeds from time to time, but it's not so bad right now."

"What day was it when you were shot?"

"I don't know. Sometime in the summer?"

"It's nearly winter."

"Huh, never would have guessed."

He raises an eyebrow. "I'm not sure if you're joking. Do you know the year?"

"Year 417 according to the universal calendars."

"That hasn't changed. So, it seems your memory skips for about three to five months."

My throat goes dry at this revelation. Was I in the indigo void for that long?

The Mind jots down more notes and mutters to himself before he checks on the machine again.

Finally, he says, "Perhaps when you are physically traumatized or near death, your ability's flight response overcompensates, enabling you to travel through the earth and end up somewhere else. Or even pass through time and space and everything in between."

*Almost like how Jack can travel to people's minds,* I think. *It's my ability, but on a larger scale.*

The Mind nods to himself thoughtfully, tapping his pen against his jaw. "I'd like to try to physically test this. To see if you are capable of it. We already know you can pass through solid objects, but what about passing through the fourth dimension or through larger entities? Essentially, you'd be able to teleport."

I stare at him curiously, having never thought of those implications. "But, when you say pass through the fourth dimension, you mean—"

"Like I said, time travel?" he finishes. "It's a concept."

I lean back on the wall, already ruling out the idea of escape using any of those methods. "Wouldn't that be dangerous? I don't know how long it would take me to pass through the earth, and I could get stuck or even end up in an ocean. As for the whole time travel thing, I'm not the smartest guy, but hypothetically, if I could do that, couldn't I also create voids and rips in space, or even conjure my own black hole?"

"I don't believe it would be that serious," he murmurs. "Though I know firsthand the dangers of unchecked impurity. Black holes are plausible. I've been tinkering with the idea. With your help, perhaps we could perfect it."

He motions to an odd metal door next to the machine he's been working on. It's just a vertical slate of metal with wires and more machines hooked up to it.

"I fashioned this out of an impurity detector while you were asleep," he explains. "Try walking through it with your ability. The machine will record everything that happens. I can process and pinpoint exactly what your body does when you transpose, and we can figure out what to do from there, if I find that my theory is even slightly possible."

I glance at the machine. I've walked through locked doors before. I did it as soon as I woke up in Kaltic. Though, under the Mind's scrutiny and eagerness for results, I feel awkward and nervous. His assertion that I could be taken out at any moment if I do something wrong doesn't help either.

*That's not like you, Travis,* I tell myself irritably. *Just humor the man. Do his experiments. It's the easiest thing in the world. Fade through a door.*

My wrist tingles where the stone touches my skin, but I dispel my jitters with a deep breath and walk toward the metal, fading before I reach it. I look down at my hand and it flickers, almost transparent. I keep walking, slowly but with a purpose.

I expect to pass seamlessly through the machine, but I crash into it, smacking my forehead painfully against it.

Cursing, I squint and back up. Maybe I stopped fading by accident? I look back at the Mind for any reaction.

Bright eyes widen in dismay. "Travis?"

Lips pursed, he walks up to me and swipes a hand through my chest. His fingers pass through the area where my heart is like I'm an illusion.

"Try going through again," he suggests.

I comply, again with the same shocking result. Now I've walked into a door twice, making me feel more like an idiot. Closed doors have never stopped me, and now a certain dread settles in the pit of my stomach.

The Mind rushes over to the machine. His intelligent eyes look it up and down, and his hands run over the wires and inspect every area.

"You can relax," he tells me while he works.

I stop fading, shifting my weight from foot to foot in apprehension as I watch him fiddle with the machine. If I suddenly become useless to him, my safety is no longer promised, right? Should I have to, I can push myself to the limit again, but I'm not at my strongest state currently.

"I think I know the problem, Travis," he says, looking back up at me with an apologetic smile. "You see, some of my machines block any compounds of the touched. In a way, they both pick up on the radiation and stop your ability. I turned that off, but the data recording is still on. Let's continue."

I raise my eyebrows. If his machines can block my ability, that means I really don't stand a chance against Kaltic alone. I shake the thought off. I'm still of importance to him. As long as I behave myself and don't act suspicious, I can find a way out.

Closed doors have never stopped me. No boundary will.

I force myself back into my fading state. If this works, and if he does figure out the logistics of my ability, who's to say he won't just kill me because I'm not needed anymore? A chill runs down my spine at the thought, but again I disregard it. I just need to be prepared and tactful.

I redo the test and successfully pass through the machine. The Mind hooks it up to a new device and starts reading the reports on its little screen. His mouth hangs open a little.

He stares at the words, then back at me.

"I can't believe this."

# Chapter XIX

## —Jack—

## Goals

I've only been in the toxic city for a few hours, and I'm starting to feel nauseous. Even though we're inside, it's still a little hard to breathe, and not just because of the air. The tension in the room could be cut with a knife. We're all quiet, a sense of doom and foreboding hanging above us.

Despite Ezra's attempts to entertain us with small talk, my uneasiness doesn't go away, not when I notice the pink burn marks that creep up his neck under his shirt and on his hands.

"So," Cali mutters, her voice sullen. "What now?"

Ezra raises an eyebrow. "Aren't you guys headed somewhere?"

"Looking for someone," I clear up. "The Cap— I mean, Alistair is helping us in exchange for our transportation, which is how we get around so fast."

I explain to them about the battle and Travis's disappearance, and how I'm unable to reach him, and I tell them about my dreams and Nora's message. Tova listens silently, leaning on the kitchen counter, while Ezra sits on an overturned crate. Thomas occasionally pipes up to add something, but the two adults seem to have the gist of it.

"You can find anyone through dreams, right?" Ezra clarifies. "Is there a range limit?"

"Not that I'm aware of," I answer. "But I have to know the person first to pull them into my own dreamscape. Travis just seems blocked."

Alistair looks up, his mouth curving into a pressed frown.

"I don't know much about abilities," Ezra says. "I mean, I don't have one, and neither does Tova. But I can't really think of anything that could block one as strong as yours, if what you say about the stone is true."

"There is a place," Alistair says, glancing at Tova and Ezra.

Tova's nose wrinkles. "Doubt it's what you're thinking of."

"I'm actually quite certain it is, unfortunately. There are no other places that fit Jack's description, you know."

"You shouldn't go. Go home instead, or wherever you came from. It's not worth it."

"We can't," Alistair says. "Supposedly, Evils are closing in north of here and from the other sides too. Even if I wasn't considering that place, it would be suicide to march back up north."

"It would be suicide going back south, too," Tova shoots back.

"We don't have a choice," Alistair snaps.

"Geez, Alistair," Tova mutters sardonically. "I bet you had a choice when you decided to leave that cushy camp of yours. Why'd you do it? For us? Seriously, Al, it's been ten years."

He stiffens. "I'm sorry. I would have come sooner, but I just … never found the will to leave. You know, they gave me a job right as I joined. It was more or less what I'd been doing my whole life—looking out for children. Things have been displaced ever since the battle, though. With the Indifferents coming in, I found an excuse to get out. No one would notice. I decided I'd try to get everyone back together. My plan was to find you three and go down to the southern port to find Yvonne, too. Maybe get a job there."

"So after a decade of babysitting, you decide to come back just because you lost your value at your camp and you want to be a salesman?" Tova says mockingly.

Alistair bristles. "No, I—"

Ezra clears his throat. "Right, so …"

"Tomorrow," I blurt out.

"Excuse me?" Tova raises an eyebrow.

"Tomorrow," I repeat. "Do you want to leave with us? What else are we gonna do here? We're not turning back, and I don't want to waste your supplies. We might as well go. But you can come with us."

"And where exactly would we go with a bunch of kids?" Tova asks, though her tone isn't mean, just honest.

"The snowy place," I say, eloquent as always. "Down south."

"Barret," Alistair warns.

I turn to him. "We can't just leave them to die here. They're your friends, right?"

"You don't understand, kid," Tova cuts in. "That place is more of a certain death than this dump."

"What if it's not?" Ezra says. "Maybe he's right. We should leave. There's nothing here for us."

"So you'd rather leave Miriam behind?" Tova snaps. "And go back *there*?"

I gulp as I look at the pained fire in Ezra's eyes that I haven't seen in the time I've known him. It's a dead light, an empty tunnel with abstract rays of deceased sunlight filtering through.

"Miriam is already gone," he says flatly. "You need to let go of the past. It's time for you to move on."

Tova narrows her eyes and grumbles something incoherent. Turning on her heel, she retreats into the kitchen. Another round of tense silence follows.

Ezra changes the subject. "There isn't much food here, so I hope you've already eaten."

We nod.

He runs a hand through his dark hair and glances in the direction Tova went. "You guys can crash wherever you want. If you need anything, just ask, but be mindful that our resources are limited."

He turns to the kitchen to talk with Tova. Alistair sighs and leans back in his chair, propping one foot on his knee.

Raising her eyebrows, Cali says quietly, "That totally wasn't awkward."

I snort and give her a half smile. "At least they're considering it."

Thomas sighs. "Jack, if this place is as bad as they make it sound, do you think it's really worth going? Even for Travis?"

"Yes," I say, unfolding my blanket and coughing slightly. "Even if he wasn't my friend, I'd have to go. Travis has a part of the stone, remember? Morals aside, we need to get that back. We can't have the liability of the stones being apart, at least to this degree. Someone could easily get their hands on it without us knowing."

***

The lights are off, and I curl up on the floor with my blanket, letting my mind wander to the conversation from earlier. Alistair's words about the Evils closing in flash through my mind, and a very specific panic rises in my chest. Why are they surrounding the area by the

Indifferents and the camp? If my biggest fears come true, the idea that the Evils are back, they might be after *me.*

I squeeze my eyes shut and reach out to the closest person to me at the camp—Nico. I have to warn him.

I find him in the dreamscape sitting on the counter in the kitchen back at camp. He notices me right away, his eyes lighting up, which only adds to my increasing dread.

"Jackie!" he exclaims, and guilt pounds into my skull with each syllable. "What's up?"

"Ah, actually, Nico," I begin, feeling worse and worse. "I have news that I need you to pass on to someone in charge."

The grin melts from his face. "Oh."

"Evils are closing in from all directions," I say, wincing. "I don't know why, just know they're around your area and you guys need to be careful. Warn the Indifferents, too."

His eyes are dull as he nods. "Right. Okay, I'll do that."

I exhale. "Thanks, Nico. I know I can count on you. Stay safe, okay?"

He hums. "Yeah, I will. You too."

Without realizing until it's too late, the dream is already fading around us, probably because Nico is waking up. The last thing I see are his emerald eyes staring at me with a quiet determination, and I know he'll be okay.

The room is dark, and near me, Thomas and Cali are soundly sleeping. Kappa stands against the wall with her eyes closed, and Alistair is dozing off in his chair. Tova is stretched out on one of the couches, but Ezra is nowhere to be seen.

I'm about to prepare my mind to go back to sleep and find someone else to warn—Nora, perhaps—when the front door creaks open, nearly scaring me to death. The figure that walks in is covered in layers of wrapped clothing and has glowing eyes. I've never been the type to fear imaginary monsters knowing that there are worse people in this world, but my wild thoughts of supernatural beasts and robots spring back into my mind.

A rumbling cough comes from the figure as it removes the layers of cloth and the something on its head: goggles. The glowing eyes are gone, and in the dim light, I can make out the sharp and pale features of Ezra.

"What were you doing?" I whisper.

He flinches. "What the—"

I wave my hand, the one with the stone, so he can see me. "It's just me, Jack. What were you doing out there?"

Ezra rests his hand on his chest like *he's* the one who almost had a heart attack. "Just on a … nighttime stroll. Just me and the city. Nothing but rubble."

"You went out in those conditions?" I remark. "Isn't that dangerous? I mean, I'm a pretty bad liar, but that sounds ridiculous, even to me."

He sighs, folding his clothes, then he plops down beside me.

"Can you keep a secret, kid?" he whispers.

"Sure. I stopped broadcasting a while ago, so none of my thoughts ever slip out."

"I don't know what that means, but okay."

"Uh, never mind. Yeah, I can keep a secret."

His breath hitches, and I notice he's breathing pretty hard and his inhalations are often uneven. His chest has this quiet rattle to it, reminding me unpleasantly of the elderly people back at camp.

"I think I'm getting closer to what happened to Miriam," he says shakily. "Everything is getting harder and harder, if you catch my drift. It's not like we haven't had radiation poisoning—a few months ago I couldn't stop throwing up—but I'm just not as fit as I used to be. Unlike Miriam, I don't have that many burns, but I don't doubt the air alone can take me out."

My eyes widen. "If that's the case, then *why* would you go outside?"

He leans back. "I know it's stupid, but I've been doing it for a while. I don't like to feel trapped, not when I know I'm going to die. Did you know that despite there being absolutely no lights in the city, you can't see the stars or the moon from ground level? You have to climb really high to find them. I do it, even if it hurts. I'd rather die with the stars than live my life blindly suffocating on the ground."

I listen to him in silence, unsure how to respond.

He laughs at my lack of an answer, then coughs into his fist. "Eh, don't worry about it, kid. I do plan on getting out of here. Maybe I'll survive."

I smile into the darkness, sighing. "You know, Ezra, you're really brave. If I realized my life had that kind of time limit, well, I don't really know what I'd do."

"We are all entitled to life," he murmurs. "And we're all promised death. It's just another facet of the cycle. It's what makes living so precious. I learned that, and I'm not scared of it. There are just too many things that matter more to me than being worried about when I kick the bucket. Like Tova and Alistair, like the stars." He chuckles. "Like ice cream. Like goals that I have."

"I dunno," I say.

"Well, knowing you've achieved everything you've ever wanted; that's what makes it worth it. Even if you don't, at least you tried. You did your best, and that's fulfilling."

“And have you done that?” I ask. The uplifting idea connects to my own plans, though I wonder when everything would ever be enough. There’s still so much to do, after all.

I sense him shift to look in my direction. “Course not. I intend to leave this wretched place, don’t I? I’ll never fully reach my goal. If I ever do, then that’s when my dreams finally die.”

# Chapter XX

## —Travis—

## **What's Real**

The Mind beckons me over as he stares intently at a paper he printed off his device.

"What is it?" I ask, forcing nonchalance and peering over his shoulder.

He shakes his head slowly. "Not, what is it, but what it *isn't*."

I furrow my eyebrows. "What do you mean?"

The Mind rubs his forehead, still baffled by whatever he's reading. "My machine was supposed to record the results and signs of you using your ability, but the readings are … blank. There's nothing. Almost as if it didn't happen."

I shrug, partly relieved he didn't figure it out so easily, and partly frustrated that there was nothing to be found; I was also a bit curious about it. At least there's still a possibility he won't just have me executed.

He whips around to face me, and I step back before he can whack me in the face. "But I saw you. I saw you walk through the block! It *had* to have picked up something, but there's not a trace. Nothing!"

My eyes follow him as he paces. I can practically see the gears rapidly turning in his head. His movements stir up a nervousness in me, and I'm not at all confident he won't snap and do something that could endanger me.

"Do it again," he tells me, his voice edging near frantic. "Run the test again."

I oblige, only because I don't have a choice.

Over and over I walk through the door until I'm exhausted. I have to focus on keeping my eyesight and hearing to be aware of him. My body becomes numb, and I can only tell I'm moving because I can see my feet take uneven steps.

The Mind runs around printing papers, fiddling with the machine, pressing buttons, and recording notes. Then I lose hold of my hearing, but the Mind notices and just waves at me to repeat the experiment again, and again, and again.

My breathing is labored, and when I touch my face, my hand comes away glistening with sweat. I halt and stop fading, willing my senses to rush back in, despite the lag.

Facing the Mind, I say, "Can I stop? Take a second for you to compare your data?"

He glances over at me and snaps, "*No*. I will figure this out."

"What have you found out so far?" I ask exasperatedly and gesture to his growing stack of papers.

It's risky to defy him, but I'm going to pass out again if I strain myself, and I'd rather stay conscious for the foreseeable future.

He grumbles under his breath and snatches one of the papers off the pile, thrusting it in my face and making me jolt back. "All the information shows that you don't exist. Meaning your presence is *somewhere else* as you transpose—"

Suddenly his gaze lights up. "Holy Pristine Mother of Kaltic."

I blink. "Alright."

He grins, shaking his head. "Amazing. I never thought a human of all things could perform quantum tunneling, especially as smoothly as you do. I still have no idea how you do it. Whether your particles shrink and separate, or if you slip into a pocket of space that allows you to pass through barriers in the real world. It should be virtually impossible for such a complex being, though I do admit the touched are some of the most impressive superhumans I've come across. Even the pure can't compete with that of the touched qualities."

"The pure, as in the citizens of Kaltic? You mean they aren't just normal humans?" I ask.

"Of course not. A normal human could never transmit souls through different mediums. And not all people of Kaltic are fully pure. Only candidates like myself and other of the Important.

"But even then, I've never encountered a touched quite like you. From the way my machines read your abilities and the radiation on you, to the way your ability defies any sort of possible explanation. Even the other touched—even the manually engineered touched, *ha*—could be figured out. Electric waves, magnetic force, things like that. But you, you're different. You shouldn't be possible."

I raise an eyebrow. "Pardon?"

He closes his eyes, opening them after a second to focus on me. His pupils dilate in the harsh light of the lab. "Are you real?"

Phantom chills run up and down my skin at his words. I want to scoff at his question, but considering my very recent—or however recent it's been since I landed in Kaltic—past, it leaves me with one gigantic mystery. Because, supposedly, I died.

But I'm not … dead. I've been able to fade all my life.

*All my life.*

I don't remember where I came from before joining that Good team, the Benevolent Blue Jays. Figures, as I was under four years old. My parents never told me what region we were from. Neither of them got a chance.

I swallow numbly, unsure what to think. It's not like I was expecting an existential crisis right now. That's not really my thing. But the Mind sure is good at making me question my life while holding it over my head.

"Apologies, Travis, that question was quite rude of me, and it wouldn't have gotten anywhere." He sighs. "I'm just so lost. Perhaps we should end this lab. I'll run more tests by myself and pass your case over to the others. I'm sure the Yield would like to see you again, so I'll invite him over. For now, I just need some blood samples."

"And what will happen to me?" I ask, flexing my fingers. "Will I be able to leave Kaltic?"

"Because of your cooperation with my experiments, I may be able to convince the Light and the Judge to pardon any previous transgressions. But I highly doubt you'll be allowed to leave, especially since you're aware of a lot of heavy secrets in Kaltic. At least you may have the Yield to help you become adjusted. That's the best I can promise you, and as a touched, it's not a bad option. You could always be executed. I am also not done with you. You may find yourself frequenting my lab."

I process his words slowly, going over everything he says twice. If I'm pardoned, I may be able to find HG again. I can't let myself be executed, so I have to continue to cooperate. Many people will be angry with me, but if the Yield likes me, he may be able to influence my fate here. Being with the Mind is uncertain because I don't know what he has planned for me, or if he will ever just kill me. I'm sure he deliberately told me Kaltic's secrets instead of giving me shallow answers, the way I've been doing, because he's confident of my confinement. The thought that he can plan my fate right after meeting me for the first time is unsettling. It makes me wonder just how strong Kaltic is.

My last resort would be to try to slip through the world like he suggested, though that is risky. I don't know how I did it when I died, and I'd rather not rip a hole in reality. I don't plan on getting myself executed. Not after kicking death in the shins and taunting it on multiple occasions. I've come too far now to just die. Again.

I exhale through my nose and look directly into his eyes. "Thank you, Mind. I appreciate it. I will continue to cooperate with you. And I don't mind giving you samples."

He nods. "Good. Thank you as well. I'm glad you understand."

After running a couple more tests and collecting some samples, he calls the Light and the Yield and speaks to them about the situation. He seems to have some difficulty explaining, but after a while, they all come to an agreement. The Mind smiles at me and sees me to the door, telling me to wait outside for the Yield to come.

I sit out on the porch, having been officially kicked out of the Mind's home. Adults and children stroll about the streets, chatting. The sun is out, casting cold shadows onto the stone road. The scent of coffee is nearby, though it smells more appealing now that I'm freezing and exhausted.

"Hey, Travis."

I flinch, looking up. My eyes meet a fierce blue.

"AR." I smile. It's not a kind one. "You survived."

"Hardly." He smiles back. "Who knew concrete could catch on fire? Purple fire, that is. I see you survived too. Lucky you."

"Right." I lean back. "What do you want? A rematch?"

"No." His feet shift, pivoting so he's facing away. "You're resourceful, Travis, I'll give you that. I hope you don't die."

"Thanks, I guess." I wait for him to say he's joking, but he doesn't. He turns his head to fix his piercing sky gaze on me again.

"I have a question, Travis."

"What?"

"Are you afraid of dying?"

"Telling an enemy your fears isn't exactly the smartest thing to do, don't you agree?"

"I'm terrified of dying," he says, his loose smile slipping off his face. "Funny, I suppose I don't agree."

"Are you trying to make me feel guilty for starting the fire while you were inside?"

"Not at all, though you did catch me off guard with that." He pauses. "I think telling your enemy your fears is one of the fastest ways to get them to trust you. Especially when it comes to people like you."

"Excuse me?"

"You're not ruthless," he says. "You could have massacred a good portion of the militia, but you didn't. You speak of your freedom like you have something worthwhile to return to. You're not evil."

"You shouldn't assume things about people," I growl.

"You value life—"

"You don't know me, AR."

"—so you wouldn't try to hold mine over my head. I can bet that on the fact that you're a kid, and that you have some morals in there, arson and threats aside. So, yes, I don't know *who* you are, but I know *what* you are. A fighter, a survivor. You do things because you have to, not because you like to."

I glare at him.

AR folds his arms. "Do you know what I am?"

"Annoying and intrusive?"

"I'm an opportunist." He shifts his stare at the snowy streets. "A realistic one. I make choices on what I think will have the most benefits. Kaltic is stable. Just between you and me, it has nothing to do with loyalty."

"And why are you telling me this?" I grumble.

"I'm just keeping my options open." He steps toward the street and disappears behind a line of buildings.

Exhaling, I try to divert my focus away from that strange interaction, chalking it up to him just being a jerk and wanting to rub my capture in my face.

Out of boredom, I study the indigo stone on my wrist, wondering how exactly it got there.

Because of one thing happening after the other, I haven't been able to sit down and study the strange piece of technology.

I turn it over in my hand, running my thumb along the tiny patterns engraved into the smooth surface. I'm not sure if it's the warmth of my hand, but the stone starts to feel hotter. Belatedly, I realize it's burning, and I can't seem to drop it. It's sealed onto my palm.

Pictures flash through my mind as the stone glows and sears my skin. Through the pain frying my hand, I learn everything it's capable of, and how it truly enhances one's ability. I see that it's almost, if not completely, sentient, connecting to my emotions and instincts to become whatever I need. I see that, and one more thing.

My vision swims, the snowy streets fading to a new scene. I'm in a wide room with adults in lab coats running around. The place reminds me of the Mind's workspace, with odd machines hooked up to more machines, and tables cluttered with strange devices. In the center of the room is a large cylindrical container filled with a bubbling liquid. Though the room is dark, the liquid is alight with its own fluorescent glow.

A woman sits by the container. Cords connected to a valve are attached to her arm. Lines of the luminous liquid trace their way from the container to the woman's arm, and her veins glow under her skin. Her eyes are closed, and her ash-brown hair falls messily over her face.

*She looks familiar,* I think.

But before I can give it too much thought, the image fades away, leaving me back on a bench in Kaltic.

# Chapter XXI

## —Jack—

## **Fireworks**

Alistair shakes me awake. His dark eyes are stormy and devoid of light, and by the sullen atmosphere, I can assume he had another round of bickering with Tova. Thomas and Cali are already up, eating some of our food. After I stretch and give myself a couple of seconds to fully wake up, I join them on the floor by our stuff.

"How'd you sleep?" Thomas asks, which actually means, *Did you find anything?*

"Eh," I answer with a yawn. "I warned Nico about the Evils."

He nods. "Good call."

"I just hope they stay safe."

Cali leans back on her hands, having finished breakfast. "Mhm. So what's the plan for today?"

"Oh, uh, well—" I turn to Alistair. "Are we ready to move out?"

He shrugs. "I suppose. Though I should explain to you what exactly you're heading into."

"Fun," Cali chimes.

Tova steps in, her arms crossed. "If you're taking them to the City, you're going to have to cross the ocean."

"There are ferries," Alistair says.

"That far south is gonna cost you a lot," she says.

He hums in response. "We'll see."

Tova shakes her head and retreats to the kitchen.

I glance in her direction, then ask Alistair, "What city? And what does she mean by 'cross the ocean'?"

"*The* City," he corrects vaguely. "It's a pretty secluded place in the south—that area you described between the mountains—but there's a whole society there. They're dangerous. And it's the only place I can think of where you wouldn't be able to reach your friend. I mean, Evil technology is advanced, but I doubt even they could pull that off. Anyway, the ocean splits our region from the south, which is pretty much no-man's-land. There's a few ports by the coast, but it's more mountainous inland."

I've heard of oceans, and I've seen a couple of my parents' maps from their scouting expeditions, but it's still hard for me to believe there's a huge body of water sitting there. Where does the water come from? Where does it go?

"The ferry," Thomas says. "It's expensive? We don't have much to trade."

"I have ways," Alistair says. "Don't worry about it right now. We have to get to the coast first."

I finish my breakfast just as a bitter yet pleasant smell wafts over our heads, coming from the kitchen.

"Is that coffee?" Alistair all but squeaks, his eyebrows raised.

"It came in a month or two ago," Tova answers, a smirk in her voice. "Another merchant. They came in from the south, as is usual. You know how it is."

"Good thing we're headed there, then," Alistair mutters. "Might pick some up from a vendor while we're at it. I haven't had coffee since we were—"

"Kids," Tova finishes, turning around with a mug in each hand.

Alistair takes one of the mugs. "Thanks. Where's Ezra?"

"Who knows," she says, waving her empty hand for emphasis. "He likes wandering around in the mornings. Says the air's fresher, but I highly doubt that."

Alistair cocks an eyebrow at her but doesn't respond, instead taking a slow sip.

Tova leans against the wall. "How is it?"

"This stuff real? Not artificial?"

"That's what I'm told."

"Could use a sweetener."

Tova snorts. "You're such a baby."

The door busts open and we all startle. Alistair almost spills the dark liquid in his mug.

"Oh good," Ezra says at the door. "You're still here. I'm coming with you."

Tova chokes on her coffee. "You what?"

Ezra's green gaze flicks over to me, then focuses on Tova. "We'll die here, and you know it. You can come or stay, but I'm leaving, and you can't stop me. Even if they're going back to the City, I'm still coming. It's the right thing to do."

Tova is silent for a moment, her mouth tugging into a downward line. After a few moments, she says, "Fine."

Ezra blinks. "Huh?"

"I'm coming too," she says, rolling her shoulders. "I'd hate to die alone."

"How morbid," Ezra comments.

"Awesome!" Cali cheers. "The more the merrier."

"Let me pack my things," Tova grumbles, casting a sideways glare at Alistair and Ezra.

Thomas smiles. "Well then."

I turn to him. "Hm?"

"They have more experience than us when it comes to survival," he says. "It's good to have them. But I can't really say I expected that."

I shrug, thinking back to my conversation with Ezra last night.

We all gather our belongings, and Kappa and Thomas discuss something together quietly.

When we're all ready, we go outside. Kappa is already waiting in transportation form with enough seats for all of us. Alistair helps Tova and Ezra climb on, and Thomas gives Kappa the command.

We lurch forward and we're off, bolting over potholes and around the rusted buildings. The air isn't as unbearable now that I'm slightly used to it, but it still stings. I'm glad we're leaving the inhospitable city once and for all. We exit on the opposite side that we came in and run through more cracked and barren land.

The sky fades from a sickly yellow to a pale blue, and the area we move into doesn't look quite as dead when sparse grass starts to appear. It's quiet, mostly, with Cali sleeping and Thomas watching the landscape rush by.

"Not much of a view," Tova says, staring at the flat land.

"I disagree," Alistair murmurs. "It's peaceful."

---

Of course, right when we think things will be okay, everything starts to go horribly wrong.

A rattling boom echoes to our right, and Kappa stops abruptly, sending us all jolting forward. Alistair sits up shakily and surveys our faces, making sure everyone is alright.

"What the heck was that?" Tova hisses.

Thomas's head snaps up, his eyes wildly scanning the area.

"Land mines," he finally says.

"Alistair," I say, "do you know where we are?"

There's a tight frown on his face. His onyx eyes scrutinize the land. "We're a couple hours away from the radiation station, but as far as I know, there isn't anything out here for miles. The port is a couple of days' travel at our current speed."

"So then …"

He shakes his head. "I don't know about the bombs. Could be set by Evils for all I know."

Thomas places his palm flat on Kappa, his head tilted like he's listening. After a brief moment, he goes, "She can't sense where they are, and I can't without getting down and walking around. Whoever put them here knew what they were doing when they set the traps."

Panic surges in my throat. I don't know much about bombs, but I do know it won't be pretty if we step on one.

"We can't just stay here, though," Ezra presses. "Just tell her to be careful where she steps."

Thomas's strained expression doesn't help calm the situation, but he whispers to Kappa anyway.

The robot takes a cautious step forward on one of her long metal legs. So far, so good. We inch forward, one tense step at a time, one held breath with each creak and tilt.

Then, *click.*

We all wince, dread washing over us.

Alistair whispers, "Don't move—"

*Boom.*

I'm flung backward, landing heavily in the dirt. Thankfully, I haven't landed on another mine. My friends are scattered around me. They don't look hurt, just shocked. My hands are scraped, and I have nicks on my arms and face. My fingers tremble as I sit up.

"Kappa!" Thomas exclaims from his spot on the ground.

The robot, shielding us from the blast, took the worst of the hit. Despite the smoke coming from one of her legs, she's still standing. Judging by Thomas's relieved face, she must be fine. And though, miraculously, no one landed on a bomb, we're all separated in a live mine field.

"Alistair?" I call out, my voice cracking.

"It's okay, Barret," he yells back. "Don't worry. We'll— We'll figure this out."

Nearby, Ezra is coughing violently from the dust the explosion stirred up. Tova rolls to her feet carefully, and Cali kneels, her hands raised out to her sides. Thomas scrambles to his feet but doesn't move an inch. Soon, everyone except Cali is standing.

"Cali?" I shout. "Are you alright?"

My heart hammers too loudly in my chest; my breath heaves too rapidly. But Alistair said we'd figure it out. And Kappa isn't badly damaged. So I force myself to have faith.

Instead of answering, Cali's arms shoot up, her hands pointed at the sky. At the same time, dozens of plate-sized objects fly out of the ground, the dirt bursting where they emerge. The mines float in midair, hovering precariously above us.

She gets up, her bright blue eyes focused on the levitating bombs.

"It's fine," she says, her voice strained yet casual, like it's no big deal.

"What in the world?" Tova exclaims.

Little craters dot the ground where the mines were hidden. Slowly, we weave around them back to Kappa.

"I can hold them up for maybe ten minutes max," she tells us. "Thomas, do you know where the mines end?"

He nods. "In about two miles. But I can't tell where they are."

"That's alright." She climbs onto Kappa with one arm, the other still extended, her gaze focused on the sky. "I'll lift them as we pass through. But we need to be fast."

He nods again.

Once we're all secure, Kappa slowly starts forward. As we go, more mines launch into the air. Soon, there aren't any more. Cali's concentration breaks a few moments after we leave the area of suspended mines, just in time. Behind us, explosions thunder, shaking the ground. But Kappa doesn't stop.

And we don't look back.

# Chapter XXII

## —Travis—

## **Worth**

"Are you alright?"

My eyes focus onto a friendly face. With the sunlight filtering through his honey-golden hair, he looks more like an apparition than a real person standing in front of me.

"You … You're the Yield, right?"

He claps and nods happily, a little too cheerful for my tired brain to process. After the disturbing dream and the stone burning my flesh—though the pain has subsided to a warm, almost pleasant feeling—I'm still on edge. However, he hasn't shown any signs of a threat. Just looking at him, I wouldn't assume he'd ever hurt anything.

And he advocated for my safety, which is my only reason to partly trust him. For all I know, he'll be the one who takes me to be executed. There's a sort of cold calm in knowing I'm one wrong choice away from death. It seems unreal, especially knowing I've died before.

Holding out his hand, he repeats, "Are you alright? You look exhausted. Oh! I'm sure you must be; you've been around the Mind all day, haha. Has he done anything to you? Made you uncomfortable? It's rude to treat such nice people as yourself like guinea pigs, though I can't remember if those are still around. Oh, but last time he had live test subjects, well, *they* didn't like it that much— Oh, I'm not allowed to say that, oops."

His excessive chatter throws me off. It doesn't help that I have no idea what he's talking about. He keeps going on and on about something or other. Since his one-sided conversation isn't going anywhere, I decide to tune it out.

I grab his hand, noting how small it is compared to mine, and shake it. He blinks and falters in confusion for a second, like he forgot he held it out to me.

"Oh, yes, that's right," he says in that too-fast, cheery tone. "I apologize, am I being too talkative? Ah, that's so very rude of me; you haven't even gotten to answer my initial question."

I let go of his hand, unnerved by how cold it is. "Uh, yeah, I'm fine."

"No, no, no," he says, his palms shooting up in a placating gesture. "The question was redundant. You're clearly tired. You need to relax. Your shoulders look so tense, I'm surprised you're able to keep such an alert posture all the time without hurting your back. You know, if you don't loosen up, you'll suffer for it in the future."

"Is that so?"

"Sure! I learned that the hard way," he says. "Come on, we should get going before we freeze to death out here."

I raise an eyebrow. "We? You can't die."

He frowns, or at least his mouth forms a semblance of a frown. The expression seems alien on him. "Ah, so you know about that … huh. Mind is more of a loose-mouth than I am. I'm sure it's fine though, you knowing."

I shake my head at his musings. I can get information later; dwelling on that now won't help me. *He* may not die of the cold out here, but I'm certain I will, and I want to get as far away from the Mind as possible.

"Well, let's go! Unless you'd like to stand out here the rest of the evening," he says, turning to the road. "Lovely weather, but it is very chilly."

I huff out a foggy breath. "Uh … right."

The Yield doesn't have a particularly brisk pace, so I'm able to fall into step with him easily, especially since my strides are longer. I put whatever frayed focus I have left into memorizing the streets and turns we take away from the Mind's place.

"By the way," I say, "where exactly are we headed?"

The Yield waves at a couple on the other side of the street before turning to me. "My apartment, of course. You may be pleasantly surprised to know your friend is currently under my supervision for a week."

"My friend?" There's only one person he can be talking about, and I haven't decided what exactly she is to me.

"Ah, yes, HG-8057, daughter of the Light," he clarifies. "The one who brought you here—"

"I'm aware."

He chuckles. "I suppose you would be."

"What's she doing at your place?" I ask, narrowly avoiding a slick patch of ice waiting to trip me as I look back at him.

He makes one of those unnatural frowns again. "Ah, she's being reeducated."

"As in …"

Sighing through his nose, he says, "I have to teach her Kaltic's laws again, reinstate our code of conduct, question and test her, use disciplinary force if needed." He pouts. "She's very enjoyable to be with, but it's very *frustrating* to teach her because she never listens. We never get anything done, getting off topic all the time. It's only been day one, but believe me when I say this is not my first time getting this job. Besides, they should know I can't bring myself to discipline anyone. I don't know why they make me do this; if anyone is forceful, it's the Axe. Or maybe the Judge, plus, she's not as *violent.*

"HG-8057 is just a very difficult citizen, you understand? I do *like* teaching her, but all my … my efforts never seem to get through. Ah, but enough about that, haha; I do have more fun aspects to my work."

He rambles on about his job, but I've stopped listening. I'm more focused on his body language, and the fact that he lied. Something tells me he and HG don't get along very well at all, from the way she talked about him to the way his voice drops when he mentions her. This friendly act he puts on could very well be just that. An act.

"Travis?" His voice pulls me back into reality.

"What?"

"Is it something I said? You were … I don't know, glaring at me. Are you mad? If so, you can always tell me about it. I know I talk a lot, so if you need me to be quiet, I shall."

I silently curse for forgetting to mask my inner turmoil. Most of my peers know me to not be the most expressive, but I'm told I look angry when I'm thinking. And despite all my acting skills, the Yield makes me drop my walls. He's distracting, talking to me aimlessly, being so lively and animated. It forces me to relax around him.

Because surely such a friendly and gentle person can't be a threat. Only, I figure that's not it at all. His I is his most dangerous weapon. It doesn't take down people directly. It earns their trust then breaks them as easily as squeezing a light trigger. I know his tactic well.

I exhale and allow myself a halfhearted simper. "I'm fine, just tired. It's been a long day. I need a break to think."

His radiant amber eyes are downcast. "You don't want to be here. I get it. I …" He pauses. "I'm not allowed to say that. I would—*I can't say that either.*" He halts, his boots scuffing the asphalt. "Hold on, Travis, I need to find the appropriate thing to say."

"It's fine," I say, mostly because it's getting dark, though I've stopped shivering. Deciding to play the optimist, I take this as a good sign rather than a hint at hypothermia. Still, whatever the Yield may be trying to communicate to me will most likely be of no use to my immediate and ultimate problems. "I do have a question, though."

"Go for it, Travis!" he says encouragingly.

"Why are you so nice to me?"

He stares at me as if searching for something in my face, then rubs his head. "You know, Travis, I find it a little sad that you'd ask something like that at all. Is it so hard to believe a stranger can be kind out of the goodness of their heart?"

"Yes." There's no thought to it; the world is just not built that way.

"I suppose I can see why you'd think that," he says softly. "No one has given you any reason to trust them. It seems like everyone has some sort of ulterior motive. Everyone wants something."

"Right."

"You know what I want, Travis?" he says after a moment's pause.

"What?"

"I want to see people happy." His tone is almost melancholic. "Kaltic is meant to be a stronghold, to keep everything wrong with the world out. That's why there's such a stigma against outsiders. I like to think I'm doing a good job here, keeping my people happy."

"What do you gain from that, though?" I ask. "Going through all of the trouble for them to live comfortable lives."

"Because everyone deserves happiness," he says. "I don't gain anything, and I think that's alright. Someone has to be the one to do it. I may not know each and every one of them personally, but it doesn't matter. My people deserve to be happy because they exist."

He stops, focusing his warm eyes on me.

"I'm nice to you, Travis, because you deserve to have someone be kind to you. You seem like someone the world hasn't been very kind to. But I hope you realize the sun isn't there to burn you."

I shrug. "I guess. I'm surprised it matters to you so much."

His head snaps up so fast, I can hear the artificial bones in his neck pop. I cringe inwardly; I've heard that noise far more times than I wish to.

"Of course it matters," he says, his voice dropping dramatically in pitch. "It matters more than you'll ever know."

"Pardon?" *That* I was not expecting.

He shakes his head, his lips held together in a loose, sad smile. "I do notice things. You glance around at your surroundings whenever you think I'm not watching. You're looking for a chance to escape. What are you so afraid of?"

"Excuse me?"

"I'm not one to assume the negative about others, but I think that if there's anything I'm good at, it's gauging emotions," he says, his warm eyes glowing in the evening haze. "Don't lie to me. If anything, don't lie to yourself.

Sometimes, you're the only person you're able to trust. Wouldn't do any good if that person lied to you, huh?"

"I'm not—" I sigh, pinching the bridge of my nose. "I'm not lying. Aside from being tired and perhaps a little confused, I'm completely fine—"

"Don't say that. I know the physical statistics. You were shot, you've passed out numerous times—"

"Okay, yeah," I cut him off, frustrated. "It's tough right now. I don't know what that has to do with anything."

He exhales out an invisible breath into the chilly evening air. "I'm sorry, Travis, I really am. You're too young to have to go through any of that."

"There's been worse," I grumble. "That doesn't matter right now."

"Of course it does," he exclaims. "To say that it doesn't means you don't care about your own thoughts. That you don't care about yourself. And, no, I don't know what you've been through to end up where you are. But you're important. Every moment is important, and the longer you ignore your limits and your emotions, the more of an impact it will bring. So, I don't know if anyone's ever told you this, ever loved you enough to say it to you." He stares at me, his eyebrows furrowed. His tone almost sounds like he isn't talking to just me, but to himself. "So I will. Wake up, Travis. *You matter.*"

I don't have anything to say back to that. I've never had an argument with someone who was fighting for me. And he's a stranger. Until now, no one has ever mentioned my importance, my worth.

On the Good team, my ideas were sidelined for action. On the Evil team, I was merely a tool used to destroy and conquer. I had to work harder than ever to get to the high position I was in, and still I was never recognized. With my new friends back with the

Indifferents—did they accept I was dead? Are they even looking?

In Kaltic, I'm alone. Except for now. For one split second, I'm found. I didn't have to do anything redeeming, and still I matter.

Cursing internally, I remind myself that *he can't be trusted.* But I don't believe that.

I snort. "I can see why everyone likes you so much."

He beams. "Is that so? I didn't say anything too harsh? Overstepped? Not even grossly philosophic?"

I shrug, grinning. "I don't know. But thanks, I guess."

"Of course, I …" His eyes widen. "Oh my goodness! I totally forgot we were still out here. Ah, I'm so sorry, we should go; we're almost there."

Shrugging again, I turn to follow him.

We weren't "almost there." We were literally right at his doorstep.

# Chapter XXIII

## —Jack—

## Biggest Leap

The temperature plummets drastically as we move farther south to the coast, reminding me of my city when night falls, though it's starting to become much colder than that. The terrain dips occasionally, and we're forced to hold on tight at times when going up and down craggy hills. Beside me, Cali shivers, and soon our breath is visible in white puffs. I periodically doze off since I have nothing better to do than sleep.

And though I'm not tired, my mind blanks out and I drift off. I don't even try to search for anyone. In these short periods of limbo, I'm caught between a relaxing nothingness and jolting awake due to Kappa's bumpy movements.

Everyone except Thomas has been napping. I watch him yawn, quivering in the cold late-afternoon air.

"How're you doing?" I ask, squirming because I don't have much room to stretch.

He glances back, his brown eyes ringed with shadows. "I'm alright. How about you?"

"Just woke up." I twist around, trying to get more comfortable. I'm wedged between Alistair and Cali. "Have you gotten any sleep at all?"

"Don't need it," he replies, his gaze shifting forward again.

"Hm? How come?"

Thomas bows his head. “I need to concentrate on holding Kappa together until the next rest break. It’s been a day since the mines, and we’ve been moving nonstop.”

“Which is why you should sleep,” I urge.

“No, it’s why I have to focus. We can’t have her falling apart.”

I sigh. If Thomas has his mind made up about something, he’ll see it to the end. I trust him. Though his ability is an enigma to the rest of us, I know he has very specific control over all mechanical things and technology.

“We should be stopping soon,” he acknowledges. He turns back to me with a smile. “I’m starving.”

---

Alistair stirs sometime later. I’ve already given up trying to track the hours, but the sun is starting to set, casting golden and fiery hues across the cloudy sky.

“Let’s make a pit stop,” he suggests.

Thomas nods and stops Kappa, and Tova and I slide down to stretch and unpack a temporary camp. Alistair wakes the others. We lay blankets in the stiff and cold grass to sit on.

Our surroundings have shifted slightly, the dusty and barren earth replaced with more shrubs and patches of dried grass. There are ditches here and there that resemble deep scars in the ground. More noticeably are the random pieces of metal and wood strewn about the land, like something was taken apart here and its pieces kicked around.

Tova picks up some of the wood, tucking the pieces in the crook of her arm. “I’ll try to get a fire started, but under these conditions …”

“I know, it is pretty cold and windy,” Alistair notes. “I have a lighter if that helps.”

"I do too," Tova grumbles, dropping her bundle. "How else do you think I'd start a fire? By rubbing these planks together? With a piece of glass and the sun that's conveniently now going away? Or with some magical fire powers?"

"You don't need to be like that," Ezra says, trying to calm her.

"I know someone who can control fire," I put in, just for casual conversation. "Travis told me what that ability was called. Pyro something or other. I can't remember."

"Pyrokinesis," Thomas offers.

"I had to use my ability on her fire once," Cali recalls. "It was awesome."

Tova ignites the pile of wood after a couple of tries. "But you can't make fire out of thin air?"

"No," Cali responds with a grin.

Alistair and Tova argue all throughout dinner, and Ezra tries to step between them. The trio remind me of the kids my age, even my own friends. In truth, Alistair really isn't that much older than us.

Nor is he that much different.

The chatter dies down as we all start going to bed. I can't fall asleep, since I've been dozing all day, so I lie there with my eyes closed and hope that pretending is enough.

After a while, I hear soft voices above the crackle of the little fire.

"You really sure about going back there, Al?" Ezra whispers. His voice is uncertain and nervous.

"We've been traveling straight to the coast without stopping," Tova mutters. "Surely you've noticed, Ezra."

"Yeah, we're going there," Alistair says quietly. "I know the extent of Jack's abilities, or at least I understand most of it firsthand. He can reach anyone through his thoughts, even if they are far away. If his friend is still alive, there shouldn't be a reason why Jack can't find him. The only thing I can think of is this."

"Convenient, isn't it?" Tova says sharply. "Have you ever thought that his friend may just be dead? And even if he was in the City the last time Jack searched for him, who's to say he hasn't been executed since? You know their policies."

"I wasn't there when Travis died, but he reportedly isn't deceased—he's disappeared. That's enough reason as any. Besides, the kid they're looking for is formerly from both Good and Evil teams, according to the records they made on him. He's got to be resilient."

"You've lost your mind trusting these kids," Tova states.

"I made a deal with them. But Jack also has that weapon everyone's trying to hunt down, and it's better for us to be going somewhere isolated than staying as sitting ducks or heading into the warzone." Alistair's voice grows cold. "It's not just that. I have a score to settle. If I can kill two birds with one stone, I will."

"I agree with that at least," Tova says. "Revenge, I mean."

"You two still haven't let go," Ezra sighs. "It's all in the past. Besides, how do you think you're going to take them on? Tova, you have no special abilities. And Alistair, you can barely control that freaky … I don't even know what it is. What can you do against such a complex and elite force?"

"I'll figure it out when it happens," they both answer at the same time.

Ezra exhales, exasperated. "Neither of you have changed. You'll get us killed acting recklessly. And after—

after we worked so *hard* to get away! Everything we did will be futile if they catch us. We're what, a day's worth of travel at our current speed from the coast? Maybe a day and a half? Then what?"

"We'll go in through the tunnel and drop off Kappa and the kids to find their friend. We'll set a time limit. Tova and I will wreak some much-deserved damage from the inside as a distraction. We'll tear down as much of Kaltic as possible, starting with the wall and the machines. Pay them back." Alistair's dark tone gives me chills, not like the cold wind wasn't already doing a good job of that.

"Do you really believe that will work?" Ezra asks.

Tova cuts him off. "What about it, Ezra? I just want my revenge. Who cares what happens?"

"And what about you, Alistair?" Ezra's voice is accusing. "Is your life's purpose as bland and shallow as hers? What about the kids? What'll they do if you're dead?"

"It won't come to that." His voice is coated in ice. "I don't plan on dying. And I'll make sure those kids get out alive."

"But we're just *walking back into their grasp*?" Ezra hisses.

Cali mumbles and rolls over. Tova hushes him. I can't stand eavesdropping any longer, but I want to know more, and if I were to "wake up" now, they would drop the subject for sure.

"I understand going in there to break someone else out." Ezra's voice is muted, so soft I can barely hear it. "But is revenge really that important?"

"Ezra, if you're having second thoughts, you don't have to go," Alistair says calmly.

"That's right," Tova adds, her voice softening. "We won't force you to come."

"Where else would I go?" He sounds miserable now, completely opposite from when I spoke with him alone. "You're right. We owe them some payback. Besides, I can't run away any longer. It would kill me worse than anything else could."

They all fall silent.

Thomas shifts, adjusting his bag-turned-makeshift pillow. I squeeze my eyes shut tighter.

Eventually, I drift into a sleeping state. I try to reach out to Travis again, hoping I'll get closer this time. I have to. For everyone else's sake.

I tried checking in on Nora before, but somehow she always finds a way to avoid me. Whatever she's doing, she doesn't want me to bother her. It's the same for Cole, when I've tried to find him on the off-chance he'll connect with me.

But tonight is different—*feels* different.

As usual when I search, the aqua stone floats in front of me. Like always, I reach for it and I'm presented with hundreds upon thousands of strings, all shimmering and loosely connected to me. These are the paths that bridge me to others. Of all parts of my ability, seeing the strings is my favorite, because I don't see who's "Good" or "Evil." All I see are people.

One string stands out. The bright scarlet one. The one that turns indigo and transparent whenever my hand goes near it. For me, it's always been Travis's: the forbidden line.

Though it's always been there, always encouraging me that he's alive, I can never seem to get ahold of it. It's like a mirage.

I reach to touch it, inching my fingers closer as if I can sneak up on it. My fingertips brush over the thread, and just as I go to grab it, it fades. My hand slips through that gap and hits a different string, one that usually isn't in my normal array.

The strings that are typically open for me to cross are the people I know. They're colored brightly so I can pick them out; the rest are white and in the background. I haven't visited a stranger of my own volition before, and yet the white and aqua swirls together as I enter a dream.

My vision blurs as I land inside the dreamscape. When it finally clears, I focus on a friendly-looking man with soft blond hair that frames his pale face, and amber eyes that would melt anyone's frustrations. He sits on the floor of a workroom lit up by fluorescent lights. There are tables arranged around the room, and strange machines hooked up to the walls and to each other. A screen in the back displays the time and a date, and while I'm not too knowledgeable about calendars, the year is one from the past.

The man is smiling, looking in my direction but not at me, like I'm not there. He says something, maybe to himself or to something, or someone, behind me.

Before I can turn around to see, the lights flicker out. My heart nearly stops as we're submerged in darkness. But it's still beating: I can hear it thumping in my heaving chest. My breath is shallow and quick. At first, I'm thoroughly confused, as this isn't Travis or anyone I recognize. I never considered what might happen if I were to get caught in a stranger's nightmare.

The lights flick back on with a disturbingly human-like screech.

The man on the floor visibly flinches. He holds one hand up to his face, his fingers trembling. He's covered in crimson, his golden eyes widening under the mask of blood.

"Are you alright, Jack?"

I sit up, my blanket gathering around my knees. I bring a hand to my forehead, inhaling deeply.

Crouching next to me, Thomas tilts his head. His chocolate eyes pool with concern, his mouth tightening into a thin line.

"Yeah, bad dream," I answer, sighing.

He sits back on his heels. "I thought you didn't have dreams. What's going on?"

"No, no, not *my* bad dream," I murmur. "It was weird. Someone I don't know."

"What happened?"

I look up, about to tell him, when I notice everyone else is already packing. Thomas is ready to go.

"Ah, I'll tell you later," I say quickly, rocking onto my knees and grabbing my blanket.

"Alright." After a moment, he smiles. "Kappa says we should reach the port today. I was able to fix her up earlier."

I grin. "That's great."

Once we're all ready, we unceremoniously climb back onto Kappa. Back to business. The dream is still fresh in my mind, and though I've seen blood before, there was something deeply disturbing about the scene. The way the man's radiant expression dropped as soon as the lights went off and on. And, of course, the blood.

Even after an hour or so, I still see the sticky red in my mind.

---

"So the ferries aren't like normal boats," Alistair explains, as if the three of us kids even know what a "normal" boat is. "They're really fast. That's how they're able to cross the ocean quickly. Though it's more of a sea, I guess, or a bay. But it's still pretty big."

"I'm so excited," Cali chirps. "Can you imagine that much water?"

I shudder, remembering when I almost drowned a few months ago in that pipe room. That definitely wasn't an ocean, and it was *way* too much water for me.

"This is the biggest leap in our journey," Alistair goes on. "Literally. After that is the final leg. I'll explain the plan when we get there, though. Right now, I need everyone to focus on the first challenge—getting on the fastest ferry. As we know, we have no money. I have a friend who works with the ferries, but if she isn't there, we'll have to sneak aboard one."

"Sounds fun," Tova and Cali comment at the same time.

Alistair only sighs.

By the time we near the port, the sun is hugging the horizon. The scent of salt and fish permeate the air as well as something tangy that I can't place. A sharp breeze ruffles our hair and clothes, carrying the sea smell and the cries of huge birds.

Before we get too close, we slide off Kappa. She transforms back to a human, and we walk the rest of the way. My feet are numb, so I shake them every few steps, trying to kick them back to life.

Finally, we reach the pier. Stalls line the inland strip where people are haggling and trading. It's not very crowded, but there are enough people that we can easily get lost among them. Parallel to the stalls are huge watercrafts—*boats*, my mind supplies. They're like buildings, but instead of towering to the sky, they're horizontal and sleek. Pipes rise from the uppermost decks in odd shapes and varying lengths, puffing out smoke into the dull gray air.

There are boards sloped up from the docks to the entrances of the ferries, and men and women, who I assume run each ferry, stand on the dock next to the planks. People board the ferries, but before they walk on, they give some sort of slip to the owners.

Beyond the boats lies the rippling sea, an expanse of gray water that stretches on as far as the eye can see. The water, moody and cold, folds and turns on itself, crashing against the port in waves. It's like looking at a liquid storm. The thought is both amazing and terrifying.

"Welcome to the port, kids," Alistair says, smoothing back his hair as the wind whips around us.

# Chapter XXIV

## —Travis—

## **Back to the Start**

"Welcome to my home," the Yield says, slipping his boots off at the door.

I don't bother taking off mine. I survey the apartment from the door. Its layout resembles the Mind's flat, though it does seem a bit brighter. The fire in the den fireplace bathes the walls in a warm light, and there are blankets draped over the backs of the couches and chairs.

"It's nice," I comment idly. It seems like the right thing to say.

"Thank you." He chuckles. "Make yourself at home. I'll have dinner ready in an hour."

"Where is HG?" I ask, still standing at the door.

"Probably in the first guest room, since she's not here," he muses. "It's the first door down the hall." He points off to the left side of the den.

"Thanks," I mumble as an afterthought, following his directions to the guest room.

The wooden floor panels are slick but not unpleasantly so, as opposed to the rough and gravelly streets that are layered with crisp ice. I raise my hand to knock on the door when it swings open and a hand shoots out, grabs my wrist, and pulls me inside.

"Travis!" HG hisses, shutting the door behind me.

"Yes. Hi," I mutter, rubbing my wrist. "Don't do that, please."

"Sorry, sorry," she says, stepping back. "It's just—he likes to eavesdrop, so we have to be careful. And quiet."

I move away from the door. "Did you want to tell me something?"

"You mean you're not going to tell me what you were doing at the Mind's place?"

"Just experiments."

"What kind of experiments?"

I raise an eyebrow at her suspicious tone. "He had me walk through a door over and over, got frustrated, and sent me away."

"Alright, well, I've heard rumors …" Her eyes stray away from me. "Never mind."

"No, what is it?"

"Just be careful around the Important," she says, her voice dropping to a low whisper. "You've met the Mind and the Yield, and they may seem like very nice people, but they're not. None of them are. They're all monsters who pretend like they have some sort of conscience."

I cross my arms. "I know the Mind is kind of sketchy, but the Yield, too? That doesn't seem fair. I know everyone has multiple sides, many different layers. And I think mostly everyone has the capacity to change. I mean, I belonged to one of the most corrupt organizations in the world, but I promise I'm not evil."

"You don't know the Important like I do. You don't know what they've done. I only recently heard this particular rumor. I used to trust most of them. But now, I can't even stand being in the same room as one of them. It's disgusting."

"How so?"

She frowns. "When they become the Important, it's not like they're human anymore. They become roles, concepts, titles. My da— The Light, he … well, he never said he was a candidate. He just disappeared one day, and then something else came back. Something that wasn't my father. I'm not even his family anymore. I'm just—just another number."

I cross my arms. "HG—"

There's a knock at the door.

"Hey, HG-8057?" the Yield's muffled voice sounds through the door. "Why don't we let Travis rest? He said he's tired."

She opens the door abruptly. "Fine."

I can't protest because I *am* tired. My senses are frayed from fading all day and walking around in the cold. I'll just have to speak with HG after I sleep.

The Yield points me to the second guest room down the hall, this one as gray as the rest of them. There's a cushy bed up against the wall and a dull red rug on the wooden floor, but other than that, it's devoid of furniture or light. There's one window, but the blinds are closed, and barely any evening light filters through. The colors in the rug and bed seem to be sucked out by the dark walls. It's different than the main area of the Yield's apartment, like the warmth was drained from it.

"I'll bring your food later," the Yield reminds me.

I nod, regarding him uneasily because of HG's words. "Right, thank you."

He retreats to the kitchen, and I close the door behind me, encasing myself in the absence of light. Shuffling over to the bed, I crash down on the mattress in exhaustion.

***

The whirling events of everything catch up to me, bringing paranoia and tension.

*"Travis!"*

I hear distant screams. I know I'm dreaming, but lately reality and imagination have been blurring their lines. It irks me, not being able to process anything logically.

*"Travis!"*

If I try hard enough, I might be able to focus properly. Everything is so confusing, so chaotic, like I'm drowning in oblivion. My brain isn't used to this madness. It's a dream, I want to tell myself, but at the same time I'm so unaware. A voice echoes around me, but without knowing who it is, I can't trust it.

*"Travis!"*

Everything is a void, and my eyes have forgotten how to function.

*"Travis!"*

*Shut up.* I'm sick of this. It's too dark, and I need to be able to see.

And then I'm back where I started. That is to say, back in that surreal indigo place with time in the stars and memories in the sky. Again, I'm standing in a few inches of milky white water, the purple heavens swirling above me in images and words. Only this time, I'm capable of looking around and standing without passing out.

Though it's all the same, I know I'm not fully here, either.

My body isn't physically here. Only my mind. I wonder briefly if this is how Jack sees things through his abilities, through the stone's colored lens. It's so turbulent and violently beautiful, I'm not sure how a child a little younger than myself could stay sane after being here as long as he must have, knowing he spent a lot of time using his abilities. I can't stand here for long without becoming nauseous.

Despite the pandemonium of it, I'm not afraid. I've always felt comfortable with my ability, and this place is just an extension of it. It's something connected to *me*.

The shouts have turned to whispers, still calling my name. They sound familiar, desperate, and I want to find them. I want to find some sort of explanation, some sort of key that will unlock the secret to solving my problems. But that's only wishful thinking.

Based upon the vision I had back outside the Mind's house, I'm quickly realizing this place encompasses the past, present, and future—an entire painting that depicts the known universe. Even then, I know I'm not able to see all of it. Can't *comprehend* all of it. I just have to try to use this space as best I can.

Nagging worries tug at me. What if I get lost here and go into a comatose state? What if the effects of this place drive me to insanity? What if I find nothing that can help me get out of my current predicament?

But I'm not a *what-if* person. I don't have time to worry. For all I know, I can't waste a second in here. I need to act, to decide.

First, I focus on the whispers. They must be important since nothing else here is persistent in catching my attention. Again, the whispers sound like someone I know, but I can't place the voice. Even the pictures that dazzle the sky can't give me a hint.

Next option. I look down at myself. Despite my body supposedly still being in Kaltic, I have the stone. I take it off my wrist and hold it in front of me, waiting to see if it will talk or light up in conveniently easy-to-read symbols. It does glow brighter, but not in the childish way I'd hoped. It drifts out in front of me as if trying to draw me somewhere else.

I step forward and grab it. My foot shoots through the pale water, and I'm falling—falling through the clouds.

# Chapter XXV

## —Jack—

## **Board**

The wind whistles across the surface of the pier, whipping over the wooden docks and past stalls.

Alistair points, leaning into the group. "See that ferry? That's the fastest one here. And probably the most expensive."

My eyes follow where he's pointing to a sleek machine sitting in the water. Compared to all the other watercrafts, this one has a narrower shape, and it's not as bulky as the other ones that have several stories.

"How do we board it?"

"Typically you trade for a pass. But we don't have enough spare goods to do that."

"So we haggle," Tova says with a smirk.

"Or we sneak aboard," Alistair finishes.

Ezra steps forward, hoisting his bag higher on his shoulder. "Let's try the first option. You really think she still works here?"

"Who?" I ask.

"My friend," Alistair mutters. "Only one way to find out. Everyone follow me."

He takes long, purposeful strides down the pier, weaving through the crowds. Bodies flow around us as we forge through. The port is huge, I now realize, and I'm glad Alistair is tall, otherwise I might lose him.

The people are all heavily clothed in hats, scarves, and ponchos. Their tired, sunken eyes contrast with the lively calls from the stalls as vendors shout prices. The port is a mix of contradictions, from the people to the unpredictable ocean waves clashing with the steady pier.

Cold sweat and the smell of oily fish mingles in the air, accented with the sea breeze and the scent of various foods cooking over pit fires.

Alistair marches us just past the ferry we plan to go on and to a small booth. A man with a stubbly beard sits behind the counter and stares at us through jaded eyes.

"What can I do for ya?" he asks, his rough voice thick with boredom.

"Does Yvonne still work here?" Alistair asks. "It's been a while since I've been down here."

"Yvonne the Navigator?" the man asks, cocking an eyebrow. "Yvonne as in the girl-who-fought-the-ocean-and-won Yvonne?"

"Yes, sir."

He whistles. "That woman's a legend. Unfortunately, I can't say she's still 'round these parts. If you're looking for her, I suggest you go back north. It ain't my business, but I heard she runs one of the ports in corrupted territory."

Thomas, Cali, and I exchange confused glances.

Alistair exhales. "Thanks."

"No problem," the man responds. "Where're you guys headed, anyway?"

"Nowhere," Alistair replies curtly. "Just looking for a friend."

The man shrugs. "Best of luck to you."

We head away from the booth, and Tova shakes her head. "I don't believe it."

"It's just a rumor," Ezra says.

"What are you talking about?" Cali asks.

"Oh, uh, Yvonne, the person we're looking for," Ezra answers. "The man said she was in corrupted territory, but I doubt—"

"What's corrupted territory?" I inquire.

"Land controlled by Evils," Alistair states. "Look, I doubt we can haggle for much without Yvonne here. She's a lot better at it than I am."

Tova and Ezra nod in agreement.

Cali snorts halfheartedly. "Well, we're great at being in places we're not supposed to be."

"True," I say. "We snuck around the Indifferents' base alright."

"We were also invisible," Thomas points out. "What are we going to do now?"

Alistair looks pointedly at me. "I don't suppose you can mind-control?"

"I've never tried," I mutter sheepishly. "Sounds dangerous."

"That's fine," he says. "I don't know when our ferry is leaving, but I saw some people already boarding, so I don't think we'll have long."

"What should we do, then?" Thomas asks.

Tova folds her arms. "If we can't haggle, we steal."

Alistair nods. "Right. Tova, take Cali and Thomas over to the pass kiosk."

Cali raises her eyebrows. "What do you want us to do?"

"Use your abilities," he snaps. "Tova is going to show you where to get the passes. Cali can use her ability to take them, and Thomas will be on standby if they're locked inside a box or something."

"What about the rest of us?" I ask.

"We try not to look suspicious and wait," Alistair says. "Barret, you use your ability to keep track of the other team."

I nod, opening a MindSpeak thread with Thomas and Cali. The smaller the group thread, the easier it is to hold.

"Alright, go," Alistair says.

Tova waves her hand for Cali and Thomas to follow, and they dip back into the crowd.

We wait a few minutes in silence. I don't receive anything from my side of the thread. Figuring I should check on them, I go, *"Is everything okay?"*

The reply is immediate from Thomas. *"There's a line."*

I turn to Alistair and relay Thomas's message. "They said there's a line."

He clicks his tongue. "Tell them to go around the side of the kiosk but not to draw attention to themselves."

Switching my focus back to the thread, I repeat Alistair's directions.

*"Easier said than done,"* Thomas replies.

*"Thomas, I found the passes,"* Cali thinks, *"but Alistair was right—they're inside that drawer on the inside of the counter."*

The thread goes silent for a second before Thomas goes, *"Okay, it should be open now. Tova's waiting by the wooden pole."*

I hold my breath, silently willing them to succeed.

"Can you tell what's going on?" Ezra asks me.

"Cali and Thomas are trying to get the passes out of a drawer," I explain.

Alistair glances at us. "Ezra, can you and Kappa secure a spot in the boarding line for us? They'll have a carrying capacity, and we can't stay here overnight."

"Sure," Ezra says.

The two of them depart, making their way to the ferry.

"How come we can't stay overnight?" I ask Alistair. "N—Not that I want to wait any longer. I'm just wondering."

He gazes at the people walking past us. "It's dangerous. There's too many people here, and just like us, I doubt any of them are above stealing."

"Oh."

Thomas's voice cuts into my mind. *"We have the passes. Coming back now."*

"They got it," I tell Alistair.

He doesn't smile, he just nods, drumming his fingers on his thighs.

"Alistair!" Tova calls, and I spy the three of them hurrying toward us.

"Where's Kappa?" Thomas asks. "And Ezra?"

"They're waiting at the docks," Alistair says, flipping through the passes that Tova handed him. "Five, six, seven—okay, we're good."

"What, thought we couldn't count?" Tova mutters as we make our way to the ferry.

He snorts. "Can you?"

"Obviously!"

"Over here!" Ezra calls, waving at us from near the middle of the line.

We join him, ignoring the protests of the people behind us.

"Hey," says a man next to Cali. "Get to the back."

She turns, her blue eyes narrowed. "Huh?"

"Cali—" I start to say when the man's eyes widen.

"Wait, you're one of the kids from near the kiosk!" He glares down at her. "How'd you end up in front of me? I was at the front of the pass line when I saw you guys."

Ezra steps in. "D—Does it really matter, sir? They're my family. I was holding their place."

The line shuffles forward.

"Dude," the man says, "you can't just—"

Kappa sidles up to us. "Is there an issue?"

The man swallows nervously but doesn't back down. "Y—Yeah. You can't just cut in front of people who were already waiting."

Cali tilts her head. "'S that a rule?"

"No, but …"

A woman behind him jumps in. "He's right! What, y'all think you're special?"

"Of course not," I say, my voice wavering.

"Look," Ezra says, "we got this spot fairly—"

"No, I don't think you did" the woman says, "How'd y'all manage to afford so many passes, anyway? You don't look like you got much value on you."

We're at the front now, the people before us handing their passes in.

"Get ready," Alistair tells our group, much to the disdain of the man and woman arguing with us.

"Only ten more spots," one of the ferrymen says.

"Hey, wait!" The people behind us start crowding in and moving forward.

"Dude, five of the people cut in," the man behind us says. "Leave them off and take the people who actually waited!"

Alistair ignores them, handing his pass over and motioning for us to do the same. The ferryman directs him onto the deck.

Tova gets on next, then Thomas. Behind us, the people are pushing and shoving to get ahead, and the wooden boards of the dock tremble threateningly.

I duck my head as I move up after Cali. The others are already on board now, and it's just me standing by the ferryman.

"Only one spot left!" one of the workers on the ferry yells, and the ferryman taking the passes nods.

The raucous crowd gets louder, their voices a cacophony of protests and shouts.

I try to move forward to hand my pass in, but I'm yanked back by the man behind me.

"Let go of me!" I turn to kick him in the shin, but he pulls me to the side.

"Jack, c'mon!" Cali cries.

The man knocks me to the ground and steps ahead. My throat closes as boots stomp around me, and I curl up into a ball to avoid getting trampled.

"He's not on!" I hear Thomas scream.

The ferry's horn sounds, and the crowd swarms around the dock, even after the ferryman hops aboard and pulls in the gangplank. Still on the ground, I struggle to my hands and knees. A boot connects with my side and my vision rocks violently as I tumble off the side.

I hit the water with an angry slap. The cold digs its claws into my skin and panic overtakes me. I flash back to the pipe room where I found the stone. Where I almost drowned.

I'm going to drown.

White bubbles rush past my face and water gushes into my nose and mouth. All I see is deep blue. My arms are turning numb, and despite the struggle, I can feel my body giving up.

Part of me wonders if it's better this way. If the world would be safer if I sunk to the bottom of this massive void filled with water, the cold and dark dragging me and the stone down with it.

And then I'm shooting toward the surface, unnaturally rising up. I launch out of the water and into the air, and for a second, I think I'm dying and ascending heavenwards. There are gasps from the pier as I levitate and then fly toward the ferry.

My eyes register Cali at the rail, her hand extended. The next thing I know, I'm on the deck, hacking up water.

"Jack!" I hear voices. "Are you okay? Jack!"

Inhaling shakily, I sit up. "Mmn."

Alistair hoists me up. "Come on, we need to find somewhere to stay. Barret, can you walk?"

"Yeah," I mutter, soaked and shivering but sitting up.

"He shouldn't." Kappa steps in, slipping her hands around my shoulders and under my knees, picking me up easily.

"Wh—Kappa!" I squirm. "Let me down, I'm fine!"

"Hold still," she says. "This is for your health."

Alistair nods, motioning for us to follow him.

I get odd looks as we pass through, though no one confronts us. We go below deck and find a vacant room. It isn't very big, but it has a table with a few chairs in the middle and a couch up against the wall.

Kappa insists I change first before doing anything, so Thomas lends me some spare clothes since all of my belongings are drenched. Cali graciously lets me towel off with one of her blankets. We all collapse, unpack some food, and pass it around while we wait for the ferry to take off.

"Thanks," I murmur to them.

It's not long until a horn sounds again, signaling the ferry's official departure.

With the door closed, we settle in. Alistair reminds us the trip to the other side may take a day or so. Thomas locks the door as well with his ability, and we set up camp in the room. It's warm on the ferry, but not suffocatingly so.

For once, I can relax.

---

The ferry glides so smoothly, I can barely feel it moving. The water passes the window in a flash, telling me we're going at speeds even Kappa can't reach.

"So, Alistair," Tova starts casually.

He hums in response from his position on the floor.

"You gonna tell these kids what they'll be up against, or not?"

He sits up. "I suppose now is the best time."

We glance at each other, intrigued.

"Right." Alistair clears his throat. "So this city we're headed to is isolated from the rest of the world, as I explained to you before. The society there relies heavily on their machines, which are able to block your abilities."

"We already know that much," I say. "Actually, I'd rather know your ties to the place, if it's so isolated."

Alistair peers at me carefully, his mouth set in a frown. "Right, so your camp is currently near the mid-southern area of our continent, and as you know, we have to take the ferry across to the next one. That's about as far south as it gets. We—Tova, Ezra, and I—came from a tiny town near the City, the place we're headed, just a bit west, past the mountains. It's no longer inhabited. Because Evils never touched these areas, they've been unaffected by their weapons and radiation, which is why Tova and Ezra don't have abilities."

"But then," Thomas murmurs, "why do you have abilities?"

"Ooh, wait, Alistair." Cali raises her hand. "What is your ability? I've never seen you use it. I mean, didn't you use it on those Evils before we found Tova and Ezra?"

"You mentioned to me once before that you could sense the stone on me through your ability," I add.

"Let him speak," Tova grumbles. "He's getting there."

We shut our mouths.

"When we were much younger," Alistair begins again, "we got caught up in this … bad scuffle."

"No, Al, tell them the truth," Ezra speaks up. "Don't sugarcoat it."

Alistair huffs. "Okay. When we were younger, we got caught in the City. There's something wrong with the people there, or at least the ones running the place. We prisoners were experimented on as part of a project, to put it bluntly. I wasn't born with my ability. It's man-made."

I blink, looking up at Alistair. Travis told us how abilities came to be, and later I learned from Cole, the creator of the stone, about the artificial element that gives us our abilities. Travis said that Evils didn't give themselves abilities because doing so was dangerous, which is why most Evils are normal humans.

My mind starts turning this over, and it clicks.

"So then," I say, "that means we can give ourselves abilities?"

Alistair shrugs. "Out of the ten of us that were captured, I was the only one to have been successful, as far as I know."

"Okay, but what can you do?" Cali reiterates.

He looks down at his hands. "It's complicated, really. When I use my ability, it's very difficult to control."

"As a witness to this," Tova adds, "I can say that it isn't natural in the slightest. He turns into—"

"A monster," Alistair finishes bitterly. "The forces of physics no longer apply to me. I can wipe out cities in an instant at full power. It's as powerful as it is chaotic, and I don't use it unless I have to."

"You used that on the Evils?" I ask.

"Yeah. They would have sprayed us with bullets otherwise." He fiddles with his fingers. "I mean, there's a certain degree I can control it to, but depending on the circumstance and how long I do it, that control thins."

"Oh."

Ezra coughs. "Let's change the subject. Uh, I'll tell you kids about the City. Since we were there, we were able to learn a few things about how it works. And most importantly, our biggest threat."

We wait for him to continue in anticipation.

"The City is run by different leaders who all work together and divide the work," Ezra says. "It's unlike anything in the world, even the Good and Evil factions. While Good and Evil are loosely held together by people trading information and fighting for a specific cause, the City is organized—*really* organized. They have schedules the citizens follow without question, their own small army, and it all fits together like clockwork. Like a machine."

At those last few words, Tova snorts.

Ezra glances at her sheepishly, then looks back at us. "Speaking of machines, the most dangerous thing about the City are the machines."

Thomas perks up. "That won't be a threat at all."

Alistair shakes his head. "No. They're dangerous. Remember, these machines can block your abilities. They have many other capabilities. Once they're activated, we don't have a chance. And if we get captured— Well, the policy isn't very pretty. One of the leaders, the Mind, controls the machines. And oversees the experiments. But with unwanted outsiders, the City is known to get rid of them very quickly, once their use has run out."

"So Travis—" Thomas begins.

"Isn't dead," I interrupt. "There's a connection. He's not dead."

"Yet," Tova mutters, and Alistair glares at her.

"Anyway," Ezra says with a frown, "if you hadn't already put two and two together from everything we've told you, the City is so deadly because of how hard it is to escape. And break into, for that matter. But we've done it before as kids, so I'm sure we can do it again." He gives us a reassuring smile. "Even the most fortified of places have holes you can slip through."

"Right." I nod. "So, does the City have a name, or is it just that?"

"Kaltic," Alistair supplies, giving me an odd look. "The pure society. City of machines."

*Kaltic.*

The name sends a shiver down my spine and chills along my shoulders. The word breathes over my shoulder like a shadow, and the image of the man covered in blood sitting in a room lined with strange machines resurfaces.

"Jack?" Cali intones. "You alright? You look a little sick. Are you cold?"

When I don't answer, Tova suggests, "Sea sickness. You should all probably get some rest. You have the opportunity to sleep in as long as you want. Unless someone bothers us down here."

Belatedly, I nod, glancing out the window at the dark night sky. I curl up on the floor with my blanket and bag, my fingers abstractly tracing the stone. It’s warm, reassuring under my touch, but a sense of uneasiness has settled over me that seems to be here to stay.

# Chapter XXVI

## —Travis—

## Greetings and the Gap

I see Jack. It's so refreshing to see a face from my past—not my childhood, but everything before I ended up in Kaltic. Back when I was wholeheartedly considered *alive* and not deceased or missing, even to myself.

I'll admit, I did not like Jack when we first met. At the time, he seemed like a brat with too much power and too little knowledge of how the world worked. But I learned that maybe he was just as scared as I was. No, he seemed terrified then. But he sucked it up and moved on because he knew he had a duty, and I can respect that.

I've known for a long time that not all of us are chosen ones. I don't believe in such fate, but it seems like the stars aligned just for Jack. But I know better now, and the fact that he carried on without such destiny is, to put it simply, inspiring.

I lurch in the air. We're both falling, though the ground doesn't look very close. He seems to see me, which is good. I keep my composure and try to straighten as much as I can while plunging to my death. It must be a dream, but I feel like I'm intruding. Or, like I was pulled off course.

"Jack!" I shout.

He looks distracted, staring at the crumbling world around us.

"Jack," I call. "I'm stuck in this city called Kaltic. Don't worry about me, I have a plan." That's a lie, but he doesn't know that, and I pretend I don't either.

He squints at me, his gold-green eyes unfocused.

"I'm able to travel through this weird void and I can see time, maybe travel through time," I continue. "I'm not sure if you'll really get this or not—if this is just some strange fever dream, or if you even get this in the present time. But, I'm fine. I never really died."

"I told you guys it wasn't the end," I say, sighing. "Once, I told Nora I would come back and find her. I promised. I don't know how much time has passed, but I haven't forgotten. But since I'm tied up at the moment, I'm passing that on to you."

I consider my next words, trying to picture the past for all it's worth. I've been so intent on staying alive in Kaltic that I haven't really had time to think about my friends. But now, mulling it over, I'm worried.

"Nora's like family," I add. "I've known her for forever. She'll try to find me, I'm sure of it. Please don't let—"

Jack looks at me oddly, like I'm speaking a different language. I suppose I'm rambling, but …

"I'm passing my words to you," I repeat finally. "Jack, whatever you do, take care of Nora and the others. Don't forget the promise."

I've said all I need to. He starts yelling at me, bewilderment clear in his wide eyes, but his voice is fading away. Soon, I'm fading away, too.

I'm back in the vast expanse of swirling indigo. I look around at the animated sky, the hazy air, and down at my feet. Behind me is a scarlet, nearly magenta footprint. Though I tried my best, I'm not sure if Jack got my message.

And I really want to let the others know I'm still here. I'm not gone or detached from the world. So while I'm in the void, I try again.

Closing my eyes, I step forward, expecting to sink through the water again. Instead, I open my eyes and see I've stepped into a hallway. The walls are gray, reminding me of Kaltic, but the place is brighter, warmer. Beside me is Nora, walking down the hall at the same pace as me. It feels familiar, but it's not a dream like it was with Jack. This is very real. I'm reliving a memory in live action.

Behind us, Cali and Thomas walk at a leisurely speed, lagging behind like they're waiting on someone. Kappa is with them, trailing next to Thomas. I note Jack isn't with us.

I glance at Nora, deciding I have to be quick. Without considering the consequences or her reaction, I lean toward her and lower my voice. "You won't know what I'm talking about. I may only have a few minutes."

She jumps. "Travis? What are you talking about?"

Exhaling through my nose, I say, "I just need to tell you that I'm fine. You'll understand later, you'll remember this conversation later."

Nora scoffs. "Travis, if this is some joke, it's failing miserably—"

"Shut up." There's a growl in my voice, reminding me of what I used to be, back with the Evils. I tone it down. "Sorry. Anyway, just listen, Nora. I'm alive. I'm a little stuck, but I'm going to sort things out. You shouldn't come looking for me. Things are … rough, but don't endanger yourself. When I'm ready, I'll find you. I promise."

Her gray eyes search my face warily. "*O*-kay. You know, Travis, you've always been kind of a weird teenager."

I don't protest. Instead, I act like nothing's wrong, like this is the time period I'm supposed to be in, before the battle at Jack's camp when we were still in the Indifferents' base. Because it's nice just listening to the same nagging voice I've known all my life. It's nice feeling like I belong somewhere, like I'm not lost.

I cross my arms over my chest. "So, what do you think about the Indifferents?"

She laughs. "Back to business, huh? I guess they're pretty cool. Very organized for a small self-sustaining community. Hopefully they'll help Jack's camp. And those Evils definitely deserve some payback for what they did to my team. They won't get away with this."

"Seems like I'm not the only one acting strange," I muse. "I don't think it's very 'Good' to be this vengeful, is it?"

She punches my arm, smirking. "I'm not a saint. But you're right. However and quite unfortunately, I'm itching to fight, and I can't do anything about that."

"Too bad," I say. "I suppose your excitement should be considered a good thing."

"Oh, so now it's good?"

I crack a smile.

Then her face starts to blur. I clench my teeth in frustration, having gotten too comfortable and now remembering I don't exist in this time. I just really want to be back. But I'm fading away.

Even though I don't return to the void, I feel like I'm drowning in that strange water. My eyes snap open. I gasp, inhaling nothing. No breath enters my lungs, no liquid, either, even though I feel like I'm submerged in it.

"Travis?"

I shudder, my body trying to pull in oxygen. My eyes dart around. I'm stuck in a cylindrical glass cage, vertical, but suspended in this white bubbling liquid. Outside of it, I can see the faint outline of someone jumping up and running toward me.

"Mind! He's awake!"

A second later, the liquid drains away and gravity takes its hold on me, dropping me to the floor of the cylinder. My clothes aren't even damp, though there's this odd smell.

Most importantly, I can breathe again.

The voice drifts back in. "Let me talk to him first."

I rub my face and try to bring my heart rate back down with slow, deliberate breaths. Tingles run up and down my arms and neck. I can't tell if I'm cold or going into shock.

"Travis?" A finger taps the glass and I focus. My eyes meet amber. "Can you hear me?"

"Yeah," I grumble, shifting back on shaky knees. "What's going on?"

"Ah, we'll get you out of here in a minute," he says. "The Mind is just getting you some different clothes."

I glance down at my shirt. It's stiff, like it was starched.

"I'm going to be let out?" I echo, placing my hands on the glass on both sides of me, my brain already coming up with terrible scenarios that led me into this situation.

It's easy. The Mind needed more experiments.

The Yield winces. "Yes, just be patient. Are you alright?"

I let out a short, winded laugh, that sounds both mean and slightly hysterical. "Sure, but what am I doing in a tank?"

He wrings his hands and glances over his shoulder. "We had to put you in there."

"Why?" My voice sounds choked, but I can't help it.

"What do you remember?"

"We went to your home," I state, my words clipped. "I went to sleep. I woke up here."

"Ah, yes." He fiddles with his fingers. "Well, it's been three weeks. Since then, that is."

I can't keep the tremor of surprise out of my tone. "What?"

"You just weren't waking up," he explains. "The Mind thinks it must be some sort of withdrawal from your ability. The Light didn't want to waste our resources setting up a feeding tube and a monitor for you, and the Judge agreed. Axe, well, I'm not getting into Axe, haha, so the Mind decided we'd just seal you away. But we didn't put any comatose properties into the tank, so that's why you woke up on your own. The Mind and I have been taking turns supervising you, and today was my shift, so—"

"Wait, wait." I stop him and inhale slowly. "So I was out for *three weeks*?"

"Yes."

"And what do you mean by 'sealing?'" I gesture to the glass walls. "What is this?"

"Sealing is a process we use in Kaltic to store living organisms," he says. "It's a bit more complicated than I can explain, and the Mind is more technical than I am, but essentially it freezes your bodily functions and preserves you in a sort of hibernating state, if that makes sense. We, uh, we use it to switch souls in the Important."

"I see," I mutter just as the Mind walks in, carrying a stack of clothing.

The Yield turns around. "Ah! Mind! I was just catching Travis up to speed."

The Mind nods, glancing at me. "It's good he's awake. I wasn't sure how well sealing would work on a touched, but the results are promising. I was also able to get some test readings through the pod monitor."

"Good!" The Yield takes the clothing out of his arms and starts rifling through it. "Hm, why'd you get so many? He doesn't need five pairs of pants. Ah, never mind."

"You can take him back to your place," the Mind suggests, standing back. "I'll give you a call later."

"Sure!"

I watch the exchange in confusion. The Mind soon retreats out of the room—I recognize it as his lab—and the Yield sets the clothes down and chooses a few parcels.

"I'll go open the pod," he says, then separates what he chose from the pile. "You can get changed and meet me upstairs. If there's any trouble, just call. I'll be able to hear you."

With that, he walks away briskly. After a moment, a panel in the glass shifts and pops out, forming a round door. I try to steady myself with my hands against the walls and push myself up from my knees onto my feet. Almost immediately, my legs buckle underneath me. I stumble back, hitting my head against the glass behind me.

Grumbling, I crawl over to the glass panel. I hoist myself out of the tank through the hole about three inches off the floor and collapse outside. My legs have forgotten how to walk, so I scoot over to the table and use the edge to pull myself up. Leaning my weight on the sturdy surface, I examine the clothing before I twist around and sit on the table.

When I'm done swapping out my clothes for the fresh ones, I trudge over to the exit, frustrated that I can't walk faster without falling.

The Yield and the Mind are sitting in the den, waiting for me.

"Hello, Travis," the Mind says. "Please sit."

I clench my fists as I make my way around one of the sofas to sit in the empty one.

"I'd like to ask you a few things," he continues, staring at me intently.

I shrug. "Can I have something in return?"

His eyes flash dangerously. "You are in no position to bargain—"

"It's only fair," the Yield interrupts, a nervous smile on his face. "What is it, Travis?"

"I'm starving."

The Yield blinks. "I— Well, of course! Ha, how could I forget? I'll get you something to eat."

He promptly retreats to the kitchen.

The Mind leans forward. "What happened when you were in the coma?"

"Excuse me?"

"The readings picked up signals from you when you were sealed. The same signals my machines are alerted to when a touched is nearby. What were you doing?"

I raise an eyebrow. "I'm not sure what you mean. I wasn't doing anything."

This is a lie, of course, but if he figures out I can successfully send short messages through time, he won't leave me alone. Ever.

He shakes his head. "Perhaps your blackout was related to your wound. Though, I have to say, it healed up quite well. Even under the medicine and seal, a wound of that caliber should not have patched up so quickly. I was told the medics got the shrapnel out when you first entered Kaltic, but even so."

"I've been hurt worse," I mutter, rubbing the bridge of my nose involuntarily. It's a habit I've picked up since I was gifted with a nice scar from being hit in the face by burning rubble. Though, that was the least painful thing that happened that day.

The Mind's eyes narrow at my quiet comment. "Is that so? I'm told the bullet should have killed you. I wonder if that stone of yours has some sort of healing properties."

"It doesn't."

He hums, clearly not believing me. I'm not entirely sure, either. I wasn't told much about it, but in all the Evil reports there was no mention of healing.

"Travis, do you have living parents?"

"No," I state flatly, brushing my nose again before I realize what I'm doing. I put my hand down.

"Ah." He exhales. "My condolences."

"Thanks."

The Yield brings around a tray of soup and bread to me, breaking the tense atmosphere. He hums a little tune to himself.

I nod my gratitude before scarfing it down, finishing it in just a few minutes.

"Yield, you can take him back," the Mind says when I'm finished my meal. "I would like to get back to work."

"Sure, sure!" The Yield trots over to the door. "Your boots are over here, Travis. Let's go!"

---

The walk to his apartment is slower than the first time. But at least now I don't feel quite as exhausted. Better yet, I'm starting to get back control of my movements, my pace steadying as we trek on. The Yield tells me I can make myself at home at his place, though it's impossible for me to feel "at home" in a place that is oscillating between wanting to execute me and wanting to use me for experiments against my will.

"Where's HG?" I ask as I shed my coat by the door.

His back is to me, so I can't see his expression, but his tone is oddly dull. "She moved back out. She's in the citizens' sector of the city, which is on the opposite side."

"Oh." *That's not good.*

"Mm." He shuffles around the kitchen. "Ah, I forgot to pick up something. I'll be right back, alright?"

"Sure."

He hurries out the door, and I hear the quiet click of the lock turning. I wait a minute before fully exploring his place, wondering if he has a map.

I make my way into the room where HG stayed. My scattered attention converges on a bookshelf slotted into the corner of the room. I go there first. My fingers fumble over the spines until something flimsy catches my hand. A piece of paper is tucked neatly between two books. The covers read *Streets of Kaltic*, and *The Factions*.

I tug the slip of paper out and unfold it, smoothing out the creases.

*HG-8057. 14:30,* it reads. Streets of Kaltic *is a good book, especially for one who loses their way.* The Factions *help explain the sectors and their directions. I highly recommend it. Sometimes there are cracks in the walls. My favorite spot in Kaltic is the northwest wall on 504 Street. I walk there every day.*

I squint at the neat handwriting, rereading the note over and over. HG's code at the top is what I assume to be a time. I suck in a deep breath and grab the two books mentioned. Dropping to the floor, my legs folded under me, I flip through the pages.

It must be a message for me. I'm not sure why she wrote it that way, but she was doing disciplinary education with the Yield, so it could be an assignment.

I glance at the clock on the wall and narrow my eyes. There's an hour and a half until the time written in the note. Fingering through the pages, I read up on the train systems and how streets are labeled in Kaltic, as well as what is held in each sector. The location mentioned isn't too far from my position, according to the labels that tell me where each of the Important live. I'll only have to take one train to get there.

When I get up, I remember my stance is still unstable, and I have to concentrate on not stumbling when I walk. I grab my coat off the hook and slip the books inside, then fold the note back up and shove it in my pocket.

Of course, the door is locked from the outside, but that's no problem for me. Within a second, I'm fading through and dashing down the steps as fast as my wobbly feet can carry me.

As I make my way through the streets, I mentally jot down the turns and street numbers. I arrive at the train station with no problem, since no one recognizes me with my hood up. There aren't many people on this side of Kaltic either, which helps.

The train is free, another perk mentioned in the books. It's similar to riding a subway, which the Evils used a lot in their claimed cities. I stumble a bit when it first jolts forward, but determination keeps me on my feet.

I'm nearing the street, one of the books cupped in my hand, when someone pulls me off the road. The stone automatically flashes into a knife, but I'm too weak to lunge.

"Travis!"

I stagger backward. "HG?"

She lets go of me, a grin on her face. "You got the message!"

"Yeah."

"What took you so long?"

"I was sort of in a coma for three weeks."

*"What?"*

"Well, I'm awake now."

"No kidding." Her eyes are stormy. "I can't believe— I asked them what happened to you, and they lied to me. Of course they did."

"Ah, well."

She shakes her head. "Never mind. There's something I need to show you."

Holding my sleeve, she drags me in the direction of the wall.

"Where are we going?" I ask, keeping my voice low.

"There's a ditch," she says. "And it leads to a hole. I've been using it for years. It's my most reliable route. And no one has detected it at all."

My eyes widen. "That's great."

"I know." She grins mischievously. "I also know how to get a map. I've been looking around. I can steal one easily now that I've been planning."

I blink, staring at her as if seeing her for the first time. "That … really helps."

"I'm just doing my part."

Finally, we stop at the edge of a dip in the ground—a drainage ditch. HG lowers herself down gracefully while I clamber down like the ex-coma patient I am.

"Through there." HG points at a small hole at the base of the wall. "It's wide enough that we can slip through."

I examine it, nodding. "It's perfect. Once you get the map, we can leave immediately."

"Right."

"Do you think you can meet me on 210 Street tomorrow?" I ask. "We need to get out as soon as possible."

"Yes, I think I will have it. What time?"

"When is the best time to be out?"

"About now, I suppose. Citizens are at their jobs but leaving soon, so when we are finished with our business, we will have the people to hide among while on the streets."

"Good thinking," I say as I climb back out, crouching to give her a hand. "We need to pack accordingly. Bring as much food as you can carry, but that's it."

"Alright." She crawls out as well. "I'll see you tomorrow, Travis."

It's early evening when I arrive back at the Yield's. Every step I take is filled with coiled tension and dread. He should be back. And he'll know I left.

I fade back through the door, wincing when I see him sitting on the couch.

"Hello, Travis." His voice is stiff. There's an edge to it I can't quite place.

I don't answer. I wait for his next move.

"Where were you? I'm not mad."

"Just taking a walk. Stretching my legs. They're still a bit weak."

He laughs, but there's no emotion behind it—that's what it is—and shakes his head. "Of course, of course. Good for you."

I lean back against the door, hugging my arms to my chest to conceal the books under my coat.

"Though, I do wonder what you were doing at the drainage ditch," he says, a hint of ice in his tone. "That was where the others went through. I never did tell anyone."

"Pardon?"

"About the hole." His amber eyes are downcast, bitter. "Well, they found out. The Important."

"Sorry." I smile. "I don't think I understand."

"It's alright, Travis," he says. "But you should probably tell HG-8057 that the hole is being patched up as we speak. Perhaps she already knows."

All my muscles freeze. I grip the books a little tighter but manage to exhale slowly, calmly.

"You don't have to lie to me," the Yield murmurs. "I can tell anyway."

"Am I going to be executed?"

"I'm not sure yet. The others … are not pleased."

I'm not an optimist. I know what this means.

I'll have to work out something new with HG. As long as I don't trigger a lockdown, like HG said, I'm confident I can get through the wall with my ability. But she has to be accounted for.

His eyes flick up to me, and there's something just slightly unhinged in them that makes me want to fade back through the door.

"What?" I ask, frowning.

"Your eyes. Why are they that color?"

A chill runs down my spine. "What do you mean?"

"They're indigo. I just noticed."

"Genetic mutation, I know," I mutter, staring at him warily.

He doesn't seem to be fully here. His amber eyes are devoid of their usual light: they're analytical, cold, and unfocused. But that cordial veil slips back over his expression, and he smiles genuinely.

"Apologies, Travis," he says coughing into his hand. "That was random. It's nothing. I'll let you get settled in."

I nod and walk to my designated room. I close the door behind me and drag the chair from the desk to rest it under the doorknob. Then I shrug off my coat and drop the books on the bed, laying them open. I search the desk, but there aren't any writing utensils.

A warmth spreads from my wrist to my hand as the stone flashes into a pen. I rip out some of the blanker pages from the books and spread them across the desk, jotting down notes and routes based on the information I have. The indigo ink fills the yellowing pages as I come up with lists and tasks that I need to accomplish in the next few days so HG and I can get out. Our options are limited, but I know that even with physical boundaries, humans are always breaking them. If we're to scale the wall, I'll need to get information on its dimensions and material. We could bribe or threaten whoever lets people in and out of Kaltic at the gate.

A tight resolve builds up in my chest as I map out plans for my escape with the device that has never once failed me.

# Chapter XXVII

## —Jack—

## **Mountains and Experiments**

I watch the dark waves lap at the side of the boat, the misty morning rising on the horizon like a ghost, blanketing the water. I woke up earlier from another new dream. In it, I felt like I was drowning, with milky white bubbles rushing past my eyes and hair. The sensation isn't unfamiliar, and part of me wonders if this is related to Travis or if I'm just haunted by my multiple experiences.

Because I never have my own dreams, I can't possibly have a nightmare. And yet, I don't remember anything except the near-death feeling of suffocating beneath water, my lungs burning.

If I peer through the window at the right angle, I can make out the erratic shape of mountains.

"You're up early," Cali mumbles from behind me.

I turn away from the window with a sheepish grin. "Yeah. So are you."

"And me," Thomas says from his spot on the floor, raising his hand.

I join them on the blankets. "It's pretty exciting, isn't it?"

Thomas yawns. "You were always one for adventure."

"I guess." Since I was little, I wanted an outside job like my parents or the Scavengers.

"So, if we succeed, what comes next?" Thomas asks, leaning forward on his elbows.

"I dunno," I answer. "I mean, there's still the Evils who I doubt will leave me alone as long as I have the stone. And Nora's still gone. There's a lot to do."

"Yeah," Cali says. "It's a little scary, but I enjoy the thrill."

"Our reality isn't built for comfort," Thomas says, lying back down and pulling up his blanket.

I nod in agreement.

"Do you think Tova's right?" I say after a beat of silence. "About Travis just being dead, wherever he ended up."

Cali shrugs. "Who knows?"

"I think the chances of finding Travis in this one spot are very slim," Thomas says slowly. "But you're confident about it, so I am too. And everything's risky in this world. One danger isn't greater than another when there's always things that could go wrong. Or right. And even if he's not there, the City seems like a place worth knowing about in the grand scheme of things, especially if they're trying to replicate our abilities."

I nod. "Yeah."

"I'm going back to sleep," he says after a moment. "You two probably should too."

Cali takes his advice, but I stand back up to linger at the window and watch the mountains grow nearer. Uncertain thoughts about the future dance around in my head, confined to my mind. And while it's better that way, I find myself much more alone.

***

We stand idly in the crowd, waiting to get off the ferry before we're inevitably swept off with the flood of people. Our clothes are dirty enough that we blend in with the others, though Kappa stands out, gleaming bronze. Her face is stony and unapproachable from the outside, so no one bothers us.

We walk away from the port, which is noticeably smaller than the one across the ocean, with fewer people as well. The other passengers stick to the port or travel different trails than the one Alistair takes us on, away from the coast and into the snow.

No one pays attention to us as we wander away from the rackety stalls in the port. I fold my arms against my chest, but the cold wind lingers on my neck like an icy sweat, uncomfortable and chilly. While I grew up in relatively low temperatures back at camp, the weather here is ten times colder.

Once the port is out of sight, we climb back onto Kappa, with Alistair and Thomas sitting up front.

"What I wouldn't give to have Thala's fire ability," Cali comments through chattering teeth. "Or maybe just a couple of layers of coats."

Ezra huffs out a cloud of white. "You'll get used to it. Hopefully we don't have a blizzard."

"There was a blizzard last time," Tova says. "I have no idea how we made it out with no supplies."

"You went through this"—Cali waves her arm at the snow-covered mounds of rocks we pass—"with no supplies?"

"Well," Tova says, "we had better jackets than you do now, since we grew up around here. But no, we had no food or water."

"Are we going to pass the place you grew up in?" I ask.

"No," Alistair says flatly. "It's abandoned. There's nothing to see. Besides, that would be a detour, and we don't have the time, energy, or resources for that."

"Oh."

"Do you even remember the way?" Tova asks Alistair. "That was a long time ago."

"I'm very much aware, thank you for pointing it out," he snaps back. "If I didn't know the way, why would I bring us here?"

"Just saying," she mutters. "I don't remember."

"Then I don't need your input," Alistair says coldly.

The rest of the ride is quiet, accompanied by the wind whistling past craggy rocks that rise as high as buildings.

***

As soon as the sun sets, we find a shallow crevice in a wall of rock. We dig out the snow to create a trench, away from the brutal winds. Our pocket in the snow and rock helps shield us from the weather, but it's still chilly. Tova gets a small fire going, and Ezra and Alistair take charge of food rations.

While I find it nice to have older people helping out, I can't help but feel useless with the adults doing all of the work themselves. At the end of the day, I'm just as dependent on them as I was back at camp.

I can't fall asleep, though everyone else has. Minus Kappa, who stands at the edge of our shelter. My mind runs at a million miles an hour, tripping over the same doubts and concerns about this quest I've brought upon us.

I wonder if it was foolish to leap into danger with half of the world bound to hunt me down for the stone. Not only that, but I brought the people I care about with me. We've faced so many dangers, from the Evil encounter to the mines. Even just sneaking onto the ferry could have resulted in an unnecessary death.

And for what? I know Travis is waiting somewhere, but this, as good of a guess as it is, is only a stretch. And even with Thomas's support, I really don't know for sure he's still alive, especially if what the adults say about Kaltic is true.

My grim thoughts skip around my head in circles, and with only the android and the cold moon and stars for company, I feel utterly freezing and alone. I have the horrible urge to wake someone up, but my self-restraint reminds me just how much I've endangered my friends already. I don't need to threaten their sleep, too.

I hug the stone to my chest, soaking in its warmth.

"Jack."

I look up, alarmed. It's just Kappa.

She crouches next to the edge where the snow dips and forms our trench, the smooth folds of her metallic dress swaying with the wind. Snow and ice stick to her frosted limbs and face, making her look like a frozen statue. Only her searching white eyes give away the illusion that she's not inanimate.

"Hm?" I answer, my voice barely audible over the shrieking wind and my own weariness that seems to mute most of my sound. Kappa can hear me anyway.

"There is something odd nearby," she states.

"Are we that close to Kaltic?" I ask tiredly.

She stares at me dead-on. Her bright eyes glow, giving her bronze face a pale, tinted look. Her expression always has an unreadable quality, stuck between something human and something not, but it's even more pronounced under the chilling moonlight.

"No," she says after a moment. "The city is miles away still. This is closer. I only now picked it up on my radar."

I shrug and shake my head. "What is it?"

"A building of some sort." Her melodious voice does not waver like mine; her tone is firm but not coercive. "I tracked an anomaly in it."

I stand up on my toes and rest my elbows on the ground surface. "Should we check it out? It could be important."

"You want to investigate it," she states rather than asks.

"It could be important," I repeat, feeling a little less sure of myself.

She blinks slowly. "It is my understanding that you are in search of the irradiated child, Travis Knight. Would it help further your decision if I gave you more information on this area I've sensed?"

"Uh, sure?"

"The building seems to be one story. I was alerted to an irregularity in the environment originating from the building. It scans similarly to the weapon you possess," she rattles off.

"The stone?"

"If that is what it is called."

I don't think twice. If it relates to the stone and it's right outside of Kaltic, then it's crucial to us. And it might bring us one step closer to Travis.

"Wait, aren't you on watch duty or something?" I ask.

"Correct. I've been monitoring your health levels and the area around us. You are all warm enough, and there are no threats nearby."

"Uh, so then is it okay if you come with me?" I say.

"It is imperative that I attend," she says. "You do not know the location, and it would not do for you to become lost."

"Should we, y'know, wake someone up?"

"That is not up to me to decide."

I glance back at everyone sleeping soundly in the rock pocket. If Kappa says there are no threats, then I suppose it's alright to leave them. I don't want to take away their sleep, and I'm not sure if they'd let me search this building Kappa's talking about.

"Okay, let's go," I say finally.

She lowers her hand and pulls me out of the ditch. With my wrist in her hand, she leads me away from the group and into the unknown.

It's not very long before we come across a gray brick building that squats on the land like a crushed tin. One wall is crumbling, while some of the bricks have cracks. The only light comes from Kappa's eyes and the stone, which together isn't nearly enough to drive away the crisp darkness. We enter anyway, Kappa not stopping to converse and me no longer fearing death, or at least, I pretend not to.

The whole place gives off a sinister vibe.

Kappa forges ahead, still pulling me along as if I might get lost, which isn't impossible in the dark. The bronze folds of her dress creak as she walks, and the sound of metal brushing metal fills the eerie silence. We walk down hallway after hallway, passing empty room after empty room. I smell iron, and by the not-quite emptiness of each room, I'm almost glad I can barely see.

Finally, I tug back on my wrist. "Hey, Kappa, I can't see a thing. Where are we?"

Her bronze braid shimmers aqua in the dull light of the stone. She turns around, nearly blinding me with her eyes.

"My apologies," she says as her left hand pops forward and a small machine rises from her wrist. It switches on, providing a lot of light and a lot more of what I wish I could see less of.

My heart stutters to a stop as my eyes take in the sight of the large room—broken glass everywhere, the plaster on the walls peeling, and most importantly, what isn't coming off the walls.

Blood. Just like my vision.

"Holy cow," I mutter, mostly because I can't find the right words to fully express my horror and sense of *déjà vu*.

"There are no divine ungulates in the vicinity," Kappa notes, placing her non-flashlight hand on my shoulder to steady me. I hadn't realized I was tilting.

"That's a lot of … That's … *that's ... blood*."

"Indeed."

"Covering the walls. A lot of blood."

"Yes," Kappa agrees.

A nauseating dizziness washes over me, and for a moment, I feel like I'm going to throw up. Somehow, by some merciful intervention or by sheer willpower, I manage not to. Looking at it in a dream was one thing. Being here in real life is another.

Thankfully, the blood doesn't look fresh, but the reddish hues along with the dark brown stains fill the room with the overpowering smell of iron.

Kappa holds my shoulder as we walk across the room, either to keep me from collapsing from terror or as some sort of comfort. Her fingers are cold and hard, but I don't mind. Having a super-powerful robot protecting me in a room drenched in blood makes me a fraction less scared. Maybe more, Kappa deserves credit for sustaining a straight face the entire time.

Like in my vision, there is a cylindrical glass container, bigger than me, though it's been shattered. The tubes hooked up to it have been snapped. On one of the tables is a chart with sets of numbers and letters I can't make sense of.

"What does that mean?" I wonder aloud.

Kappa analyzes the paper. "It's a code. It says, 'Purity experiment tests. These notes are not for citizens to read. I am here with an associate trying to manufacture a new compound that can safely upgrade the pure, untouched, and touched. We are trying not to harm the subjects, but I am told pain is necessary to continue the tests.

"'Test one is successful, though a new element was not created. Instead, remnants of the old radiation from the outside world were used directly on a patient, giving said subject strange capabilities affecting gravity and electricity. Tests two through nine were unsuccessful, though every patient made it out alive. Test ten is the most successful in creating the chemical, though the effects haven't been shown yet. New element is a dark indigo liquid instead of the usual blue or green solid or plasma, and it seems to be very unstable, though patient has survived. Patient, however, is not exhibiting signs of super abilities.'"

"Stop, stop, stop, stop," I say, holding up my hands.

Kappa glances away from the notes. "Yes?"

I shake my head, muttering, "Ten tests. Ten people in total. Alistair mentioned being captured. But … indigo. Could Travis have anything to do with this? I don't understand."

"Perhaps we should take this chart?" Kappa offers.

"Yeah, that's a good idea."

I feel like I'm closer to bridging the gap—the hole where an answer is supposed to go. Even though I don't know everything, it all feels connected, from Travis to Alistair to Kaltic.

If anything, I'm sure Alistair knows what this means. It's more than a hunch—I'm *sure* he knows what this is. The only doubt I have is whether he'll actually answer my question if I ask.

When we get within sight of our resting place, I see Thomas frantically walking around the pit and pacing up and down in the snow. He spots us and runs toward us, his heels kicking up snow.

"Where the heck were you?" he exclaims. "I thought I might have had a stroke when I saw you both missing."

"I don't think that's how it works," I comment.

"It isn't," Kappa says.

"*That*— That's not the point!" He inhales slowly, his breath rattling. "Answer my question. Where were you two?"

"We were checking out an abandoned lab close by," I say, trying to ignore the heaving gulps he takes, the way he seems both relieved and close to losing it.

Thomas shakes his head. "Why didn't you tell anyone?"

Kappa stands beside me saying nothing, like the helpful accomplice she is.

"You were all sleeping so well … and I thought it was important."

"*It doesn't matter*," he hisses. "You both should have better common sense."

I open my mouth to object, but Kappa holds out her hand in a *wait* gesture.

"I apologize, Thomas, but I am fully capable of taking care of myself and Jack. There are no other human life forms around; we would not have been harmed." She turns to me. "Was the information not important?"

I blink. "Maybe we should wait for the others to wake—"

She thrusts out the documents into Thomas's chest. "These are notes regarding experiments. I will recount them to the group if you so desire."

Thomas only stares, stunned.

Kappa pats him on the shoulder and walks past him to stand on the other side of the ditch and watch the dawn horizon.

I lower my head. "Thomas, I'm sorry we didn't say anything. This is really important, though. Even if it has nothing to do with Travis, we can take these notes back to the Indifferents—"

"I get it," he says quickly, smiling wanly. "It's fine. Saving the world is your priority, right? I'm sure I'll never stop losing sleep over your crazy antics. That's what I agreed to when I decided to go with you. So, it's fine."

I want to argue with him. To tell him that it's much more personal than just saving the world. That I'm way more loyal to my friends and family—that those special people are my priority, and that the world will have to come second. But I can't. I can't risk another fight, and I'd rather live in remorseless guilt than ruin my friendship.

# Chapter XXVIII

## —Travis—

## **Revelations**

It's been four days since I came out of the sealing pod and completely ruined HG's plans. She dropped by a few times to exchange books with me and the Yield, and once with the excuse that she had baked a cake, which she had. She slipped me the map inside a book, and we traded more notes that way, too.

In one of her first notes, she told me she knew what had happened—how we were seen and reported by the Secretary without knowing it. I sent her back a copy of the notes I'd made soon after, so we could finalize the plan.

With my door jammed, I used my knife to create a pocket inside one of my boots to slip the map into, so I can keep it on me at all times.

I work furiously at night after collaborating with HG. She wrote that with the right bribe, she might get a guard to open the gate for her. But not me.

So she sent me a piece of the wall, stolen from one of the Important's offices. Luckily, it's just stone, not metal or any machine, and I figure I can fade right through it with the stone.

Tomorrow is my last full day in Kaltic, and the morning after is when we escape. Over the past few days, the Yield has tried to regain my attention. I do my best to humor him, knowing that he is one of the main reasons the other Important haven't executed me yet. But I can't be too nice to him and risk slipping up.

The Yield is mostly lenient with me, which I have to appreciate, since he's feeding and sheltering me while I work behind his back.

It bothers me that he's so kind, but I have to detach myself from whatever emotion I might have, whatever grateful friendliness I've developed just because he's been nice to me. If I fall under the notion that he's my friend, it will be that much harder to betray him in the end.

I'm done betraying my friends. HG, I've decided, is trustworthy. I consider her an ally completely. Friends are hard to come by, especially in my case. For a long time no one really liked me.

The pathetic memories of my childhood are almost laughable. I recall times when other children avoided my questions and chose to ignore me when I spoke. Even in my Good team, I was often left out of their activities. Mostly because, admittedly, I've never been much fun.

They told me I was too serious and kind of weird, and I'd always tell them they were immature and idiotic. I'd remind them we were in the middle of a war. That being said, they stopped speaking to me after a while. Nora wasn't like them. Either she didn't know I was supposed to be the child recluse, or she genuinely found me interesting enough to spend time with. And then, she ended up being my only friend. I pretty much grew up with her, and to say we're still close would be an understatement. She learned to read my moods, and I learned to adapt to her phases.

It wasn't exactly hard to cut ties with my Good team, but months after, I still regretted leaving Nora. My parents had died, so she was the only one I had. And yet, I needed change more than comfort. I wanted to find my place. I joined an Evil team, worked and manipulated my way into a high position, and found two allies in Natasha and Rowan. They were friends.

Not everyone labeled Evil is corrupt. Some were born into the side, others too scared to go anywhere else. Natasha wasn't evil. She shared her supplies with me when I first joined. Rowan wasn't evil, either. He taught me how to use a gun and helped me when I struggled.

But I killed Natasha, and Rowan attempted to kill me, so I can't really say much about our relationships.

And then there's the golden trio—Jack, Thomas, and Cali. I trusted them at one point, didn't I? They're younger than me, but not by a lot, and they're actually tolerable. They're resilient. For their lack of understanding of the world, they understand what it's like growing up in tough conditions. And when I was in my hour of presumed death, they were there, too.

Most people don't have siblings. The rate of single children has only gone up with time. I envied Jack that he could have that kind of bond with his brother, to the point where he'd *die* for him. Now, considering that, I'm glad I don't have anyone extra to stress over.

"Travis!" A singsong voice calls into the stillness of the kitchen where I'm sitting, content for the moment with just my thoughts and a piece of toast.

I sigh through my nose.

The Yield skips in. Smiling, he fixes his warm amber eyes on me.

"I've been thinking," he starts.

I wait, glancing up at him.

"You've been planning to leave," he continues.

Coughing, I look up, barely managing to keep my surprise under control. "What?"

He shakes his head. "You don't have to be cautious around me. The other Important … They're deciding your fate."

I don't answer.

"That being said, I haven't really been telling you things either. Mostly because I am simply not allowed to." His eyes catch a mischievous glint. "Whatever. When has anyone followed every rule? I don't really care about those things; they're quite boring."

"What are you implying?" I ask.

"There isn't much I can do for you now, other than tell you the truth." He smiles sadly.

I raise my eyebrows, prompting him to continue.

He looks around, then presses some sort of panel in his wrist, turning a device off. A microphone or sound monitor, I assume.

"Years ago, I don't really remember how many, we had a series of experiments. The Mind and me. Yes, we're good friends, and we wanted what was best for the people of Kaltic. He wanted to upgrade the pure, and I wanted to keep them safe. Somehow, he convinced the Axe to go on an expedition for him and find ten subjects. These subjects could not be one of the touched.

"She came back with ten untouched humans: nine children and a young woman who seemed to be their supervisor. They did not agree to the experiments, but the Mind did not care. It was for the better good, he'd always say. I believed him." The Yield pauses, sighing.

"Go on," I say, hoping I don't sound too apathetic but also not too intrigued.

"We didn't know the woman was going to have a child," he says, his expression pained. "If I'd known, I would have done something. No, I should have done something from the beginning! They were children, *innocent children*, and I knew this. Long ago, a great inventor manufactured an element from the same compounds that cause impurity in humans. Abilities. The Mind wanted to do the same, to recreate it, but in a way that the chemical interacted with untouched people without the risk of death. He wanted to turn the pure, people like me, and the untouched, the people of Kaltic, into a new race of superhumans.

"I thought it was a great idea. I thought perhaps we could advance our race. Instead, we created a monster. The rest of the tests failed, but none of the subjects died. We thought, maybe, we were close to getting successful results. The first test, a fiasco, yes, but the rest were proving to be more promising. Our last subject was the woman. We repeated the first test, but with the Mind's prototype element. It didn't seem to do anything. But now, it seems it did."

I sit forward, my mind already knitting together the pieces of his story. But I need confirmation. "You're telling me this because …"

He brushes back his hair. "Don't you understand, Travis? Of course, you weren't there in person. But the element, the physical chemical we made—it was the same color as your eyes. Could it be a coincidence? Yes, indigo is a rare mutation in iris coloration. But you'll have to believe me when I say you look exactly like your mother."

# Chapter XXIX

## —Jack—

## Arrival

The sun rises and the snow sparkles on the ground. Towers of rock loom over us on both sides of the valley, shadows flitting between the sun and clouds. We eat a quiet breakfast, swallowing our anxiety with some lukewarm coffee on the side.

Finally, when I'm more impatient and less nervous, I present the notes to Alistair and the others, asking Kappa to translate.

Alistair's eyes widen with each sentence, and he keeps glancing at Tova and Ezra. Thomas sits forward, now interested. Cali makes a snowman with her ability, half listening.

Alistair holds out his hand to stop Kappa before she finishes.

Staring at him expectantly, I say, "Well, what does it mean? You know what this is, don't you?"

"Where did you find this?" he asks.

"Kappa and I went investigating this building she sensed."

His eyes widen. "We're a lot closer to the City than I thought, then."

Tova grunts. "Well, we have transportation. Back then, we walked."

"Cap— Alistair!" I say. "The charts. What do they mean?"

"Exactly what they sound like." He folds his arms. "Remember, I said ten of us were captured. Those notes describe what happened. The first experiment is talking about me, if you hadn't guessed."

"Right, right." I pause. "Do you think we should just destroy the notes?"

Thomas's eyes widen. "Why would we do that?"

"Well, think about it. Everyone will want this, but more harm than good could be done if the information reaches the wrong people."

Thomas frowns. "True, but—"

"You can't throw that away," Tova butts in. "It's proof of Kaltic. So what if the information gets out? That's the one thing they're scared of—being found. It would be the perfect revenge."

"I don't know, Tova," Alistair murmurs. "That's taking it too far."

"How so? I thought you wanted to destroy Kaltic."

"Not at the cost of leaking information that would give the Evils the power to manufacture abilities and destroy everything else," he says. "It's not worth it."

"So you're not getting revenge," she states.

"I didn't—"

"Have it your way," she mutters darkly. "It's probably for the best."

No one says anything about Ezra's sigh of relief, though inwardly, I'm glad too. Revenge sounds too messy for our original purpose anyway.

---

Kappa forges through the snow, her legs sinking with every step. The ride is especially bumpy, and we have to stop a couple of times so Kappa can dig herself out of the slush.

"So, there's a tunnel on the northwest city wall that connects to a drainage ditch," Alistair says, his blond hair whipping around his eyes as he stares at the expanse of white and gray. "It should be big enough for everyone here to slip through. That's how we get in. If I remember right, that area is where he's being held as an intruder, though I'm not sure which building he could be in. Try to follow the wall. We might be here a while looking for him, so don't get caught. Try to blend in with the citizens, and if someone stops you, tell them you're lost and ask for directions to the northwest train station."

We nod.

"I'll make sure you don't get caught by the militia," Alistair continues. "If things start going south, I need everyone to book it out of there. Run back to the tunnel. Don't stop for anyone or anything, even if you don't find your friend. If you get caught inside the City while it's on lockdown, the chances you'll be able to escape drops."

"So, if this place blocks abilities, will we still be able to use ours?" I ask.

"You should, unless it's put on lockdown. You'll know if that happens," he says. "This plan depends entirely on the odds that we don't get caught, so try your best to be sneaky and quick. You'll have to play a lot of this by ear."

"If we have to split up, I can create a link for all of us to communicate in," I suggest. "Y'know, with my ability. It won't be hard reaching everyone here. I'll try to call for Travis with it as well."

"Alright, sounds good," Alistair says.

Through the winter flurry, rising gray walls and buildings shine in the morning light, the sun reflecting off the icy city of machines.

We're here.

# Chapter XXX

## —Travis—

## The Yield

My head is spinning, and once again, I'm at a loss for words. The Yield's eyes are downcast, focused on the table as he recounts the remainder of the story—how the kids escaped using the ability of the first experiment.

"The boy we turned into a monster came back for the woman, who I believe is your mother," he says. "We were keeping her in a lab outside of the city. I was there at the time, with a team of the Mind's engineers and scientists.

"I—I made a mistake. I had let the children integrate into Kaltic, so they were technically my citizens. But the boy came back, very unstable, and threatened to destroy the lab and everyone inside to get the woman. I was stupid to think things could be resolved peacefully."

He laughs softly, a bitter, self-deprecating noise.

I wait for him to finish, willing myself to focus, but my mind keeps going over the same idea—my mom is connected to Kaltic. My ability is connected to Kaltic.

"I told him to think about the path he was choosing," the Yield continues. "I thought it wasn't my right to stop him and defend my citizens, nor actively betray my city by helping him leave peacefully. So, I sat and closed my eyes. Some of the smarter citizens ran, but the majority stayed loyal. And he slaughtered them."

"I'm sorry," I say because it seems appropriate.

“Me too,” he mutters. “But I suppose you would never be the person you are today had that not happened. Funny how you ended up back here, only to try to do the exact same thing—leave. The Mind would go ballistic if he knew you were the product of all of his hard work and you managed to slip away. Guess it can’t be helped, especially since he’s giving up.”

We sit in silence.

It’s as if the missing portion of my life has been filled in. The whole reason I exist ties back to Kaltic, and it makes sense that I ended up here in my time of “death.” However the element works, just like the stone, it must have its own level of sentience. My ability brought me back to the place it was created.

I died and literally met my Maker.

*He’s giving up.*

If the Yield can’t advocate for me, and the Mind is no longer holding on to the project, then I’m as good as dead. If I don’t escape, that is. The plan’s timing couldn’t have been better.

“You know, Travis,” the Yield says so softly I almost don’t hear him. “I really do love my people. I love them so much it hurts, which is preposterous since I can’t feel real pain in this body. I’m … I’m not a warrior like the Axe, but I would kill for my people. But when it comes to them, to my citizens, I let them choose. In Kaltic, the laws are wired to create as little room for choice as possible, but I let them get away with loopholes because I believe in self-made decisions.

“So, back then, I let that boy choose. And I let the scientists choose. But ultimately, I made the choice to stand by.” He pauses, a sad smile twisting onto his face. “Imagine allowing your children to kill each other.

"I opened my eyes and found myself alone. I thought to myself, 'This is fitting; this is exactly what I deserve.' Because, Travis, I made a decision. And now I will make the same decision. I'll let you choose what you want to do." His eyes are glossy. "I know you want to leave Kaltic, but temporarily, allow me to say, welcome home."

I crack a half smile at the irony of being welcomed to a place I planned to leave from the beginning, though the original thought of here being the place that made me still hits hard.

He blinks, then smiles too. "Right, enough of that. I have work to do, and I'm sure you do, too. I'm sorry I can't do anything more, but I can at least warn you of what the other Important decide to do with you when they've made their final decision."

With that, he gets his coat and leaves.

---

After the day has settled into evening, HG meets up with me in the alley by the Yield's flat to run through our final plans of escape. I'm not waiting for the Important to finally decree my execution. Over the past few days, I learned multiple routes to the rendezvous point. I've plotted my way there so much, I could probably do it with my eyes closed.

Of course, it's tonight that the Yield confronts me again, dealing the last blow to whatever morale I've stored up.

"You're not going to quit, are you?" he asks during dinner. "Trying to leave and all."

I avoid his gaze. "No."

His smile is one of those slightly miserable ones that I've been seeing more often. "I'm sorry about your experience in Kaltic. I wish things could change."

"Why can't they?" I ask, stirring my food around.

"Because it would ruin the design," he answers. "Kaltic would no longer be the safe place we created."

"Freedom doesn't guarantee safety. It's the risks in our choices that make it all worth it," I say. "You're suffocating your people."

He looks like I stabbed him. "A utopia could never run properly if the people had that," he says softly. "Freedom. They would never be satisfied."

I don't have anything to say in response, so I don't answer.

He drops his head in his hands. "I just want them to be happy. They're my people, and they deserve the world. But if I give them the world, they'll suffer."

"Some things are worth suffering for."

"You sound like you know from experience."

I shrug, then think back to my conversation with HG about the Important. About how inhuman they are. And yet, the Yield sounds more human than a lot of people I know.

"I have a question," I say, recalling HG's words.

"Yes?"

"Do you see your people as numbers?"

"Wh—What? Of course not …"

"Oh?"

He lifts his head, eyebrows furrowed. "You know, a long time ago, when Kaltic was first founded, people still had real names like yours. Now we distribute codes to make it easier to keep track of citizens. I hate the codes. They're impersonal. But I use them anyway. We have to. Names are important, and we wanted everyone to be born equal."

"Do you remember the name of the original Yield?" I ask.

He smiles. "Isaiah."

I nod. "It's fitting."

"Isaiah's memories are old. But sometimes, when I feel down, I revisit them because they're the happiest," he says. "Isaiah was filled with hope. He saw Kaltic as a place he could build to save people. He loved humanity, despite the terrible things humans are capable of."

I set my fork down. "You're Isaiah too."

"Maybe." He sighs.

We eat in silence after that.

He's no longer "the Yield" to me. It doesn't make sense. To yield means to give way. But he's more than that. He's confident, and he doesn't allow Kaltic to boss him around. He breaks the rules whenever he feels like it. The Yield isn't a name.

He's Isaiah.

After dinner, I gather the things HG lent me and put them in a satchel. It's not much, just my extra clothes and, of course, the stone. But that stays on at all times.

Sitting on my bed, I go over and over the plan to meet with HG under the cover of the citizens as soon as the first bell for the morning rally chimes. Together we'll use the winding route to get us to the gate. HG has bribed the guard up there before to let her take a short walk outside. I'll stay back while she goes out, then I'll fade through the wall. If the guard doesn't let her out, I suppose I'll have to fight. Then we'll make a run for it. We'll use the map HG swiped to figure out our bearings and how to get out of the mountains. From there, we'll find the port I saw marked on the map.

It has to go smoothly. If I'm caught doing this, there will be no more question over my death. I'm an established threat to Kaltic, and even the Yield—Isaiah—can't stall for me.

Isaiah appears in the doorway, clutching a piece of clothing. His small frame and soft eyes remind me of his humanity, how he's just a normal man at the end of the day.

"Yes?" I say.

He steps forward, handing me the coat he gave me when I first ran into him.

"You know it gets really cold out there," he says, running a hand through his hair. "It fits you anyway, right?"

I take the coat, unsure of myself. "Why are you giving me this?"

"They've decided."

"It's bad?"

"Yes. The execution is tomorrow at noon."

Before I can say anything else, he gives me a tight hug. I don't protest, not wanting to ruin the moment for him. His arms are strangely warm despite him not being a human, and when he releases me and steps back, I meet his eyes blazing with determination.

"One day things will change for Kaltic," he tells me. "Whether soon or in centuries. Even when all that's left of me are my memories and a new Yield has come along to take my place, he'll know what it all means, what sacrifices must be made. I'm sorry it's come to this, but we won't forget you. The impact you made."

With that, he turns to leave.

"Hey, Isaiah?" I call.

"Yes?"

"Thank you."

Isaiah falters, remorse hanging over him like a cloud. "Why?"

I shrug. "Because you didn't give up on me."

He gazes at me from over his shoulder, granting me the trademark smile that's so full of sunshine and life, though it's twisted now with guilt and sorrow.

"I wish you could be free, Travis."

# Chapter XXXI

## —Jack—

## **Monster**

Our boots crunch in the snow as we approach the wall on foot.

"Everyone remember the plan?" Alistair asks.

"It's a pretty terrible plan, but yes," Tova says.

He raises an eyebrow. "Did you have something better in mind?"

"No, just making sure you're aware your plan sucks," she replies. "This whole situation sucks; your plans won't be spared."

"You can wait out here in that case," he shoots back.

"I have to supervise you."

"If you two old ladies would kindly stop bickering and get to the point," Ezra cuts in, "that would be greatly appreciated."

Alistair huffs. "Alright, everyone see that hole there?" He points at the bottom of the wall where a gap barely peaks through the piled snow.

"Uh, no?" Cali says.

Tova crosses her arms. "We'll dig out the way."

We all work together to clear the opening. Our spirits plummet, crashing and sinking into the snow, when we find a hole that's blocked off by a grate with metal slits about as big as my finger.

"Is it … supposed to be like that?" Cali asks in a small voice while Thomas crouches down to inspect it.

"It's been sealed off," Ezra murmurs.

"We can break it, though, right?" I say, panic creeping into my throat. "Kappa can, maybe?"

Thomas shakes his head. "Even if we were to get the grate off, the tunnels down there are probably blocked too." He glances at the adults. "If you were able to fit through it before, then it's been tampered with. There's no way we could get through."

Tova huffs. "Alright, well, we tried. Let's go home."

I ball my fists. "No! We already came so far. There has to be another way."

Cali kicks at the wall, her brows furrowed. "Can't we just, I dunno, climb it?"

Thomas frowns, glaring up at the stone towering high above us. "With what gear? I don't know about you, but I doubt I'd be able to make it to the top."

"Yeah, it looks like it's over a hundred feet high," Ezra muses.

We can't just stop here. Not after everything we went through to get here, knowing Travis could be somewhere beyond the wall. I won't allow it.

"Alistair!" I whirl around to him, desperate. "Please, there has to be something we can do."

His mouth is drawn into a thin, solemn line. "I'll see what I can do."

"Al, you're not seriously planning—" Tova cuts herself off. "Think of everything that can go wrong!"

"No." His tone is firm and resolute. "I have an idea."

Tova sighs, running her hand down her face. "Great."

Alistair takes a step closer to the wall, then holds his hand out. "Everyone stand back, please."

We do as he says. He plants his feet in the snow and cracks his knuckles. A wind whips harshly against us, bringing with it a flurry of snow. The ground around us rumbles, and more powdery snow flies up, temporarily blinding me. I stumble and fall as another tremor shakes the earth.

"Let's hope that didn't raise any alarms." Alistair's voice rises from the direction of the wall. We all trudge forward as the temporary blizzard dies down as quickly as it started.

And then the ground drops from beneath me, and I'm slipping in the wet snow and tumbling down a harsh incline that was definitely not there before.

"Jack?" Cali calls.

"Ah, sorry," Alistair says. He's standing near me at the bottom of this shallow ravine. "Everyone be careful coming down, it's a bit steep."

"Coming down?" Thomas repeats.

I roll onto my elbow and shake the snow off me. Alistair holds a hand out to help me up. I take it gratefully. I turn around and face the wall, or, what I assumed was the wall.

The others slide down into the crack in the earth that stretches under the gray stone we were once facing. Between pillars buried deeper in the ground is a space big enough for us to squeeze through. Overall, the hole isn't very big, only a few feet deeper than the actual wall.

"You … did this?" Thomas gazes at the passageway with awe.

Alistair hums. "Yeah. Come on."

We follow Alistair under the wall, crawling underneath the cold patchwork of stone and metal, and out to the other side where we end up in some sort of ditch. The ground around here is cracked; little fractures snake along the pavement.

Crouching in the ditch, I open a MindSpeak thread with the group so we can be silent.

*"Alright, just think through here,"* I tell the group.

*"Like this?"* comes Tova's voice ringing in my head.

*"Yeah. Keep it to a minimum."*

*"I think Tova and Ezra should stay here in the ditch,"* Alistair decides, picking up the thread easily.

*"Why?"* Tova asks.

*"You can watch our bags. We shouldn't travel in a big group,"* he explains.

*"What if someone comes by while you guys are gone?"* Ezra asks.

*"I'll leave Kappa with you as a precaution,"* Thomas says.

*"Fine,"* Tova acquiesces. *"Go beat them up for me, Al."*

"I decline," Kappa says out loud, having access to the thread but the inability to use it.

*"That's an order, Kappa,"* Thomas says sternly. *"You guys have to be our backup when we come back."*

Rather than reply, she leans back on her heels and folds her arms.

*"I want you to run back outside the city with our stuff at the first sign of trouble,"* Alistair tells them. *"But we'll need you here inside to help us if something goes wrong and any one of us is injured. If someone dangerous sees you, run to the dumpster alley near here—you guys know the one."*

*"Roger that, Captain."* Tova flashes a grin and mock-salutes. *"We'll be waiting, so you'd better come back."*

*"I'll check if the coast is clear."* I grip the edge of the ditch, pressing myself against the cool wall. Stretching upward ever so slightly, I peek over the side. The streets are snowy, the sun sparkling on the stone.

Along the streets, brick buildings line up, matching the peaceful picture I saw in a dream.

I release the edge and turn back to the others. *"We're good."*

Alistair nods, then gestures for us to follow him, and we climb out of the drainage ditch. Tova, Ezra, and Kappa stay behind, crouching in the shadow of the wall with our bags.

We creep behind one of the buildings and look around, gaining our bearings in the shiny winter city.

My head pounds with the exhilaration of finally finding Travis again. It's odd how I can just sense he's here. It's more than a gut feeling—it's elation—knowing he can't be far and this journey will have paid off.

We sneak out of the alley we emerged from, following Alistair, who insists on walking ahead of us so he can warn us of danger. The streets are devoid of life, reminding me eerily of the empty roads back in my city, marking a ghost town. But the clean pavement and polished wooden doors of the spectacular brick buildings say otherwise.

Right now, however, it's just the solemn buildings, the lightly falling snow, and our own soft footsteps.

*"This place is cool,"* Cali notes in the thread.

*"Cali,"* I chide, *"don't use it for casual conversation."*

*"Sorry, I wasn't really thinking about it,"* she goes.

No one else speaks, or, well, thinks aloud.

Thomas looks distracted, his eyes darting around to glance at the doors, the walls, from left to right and over his shoulder behind us.

*"Is something wrong?"* I ask him.

*"Nothing,"* he replies quickly. *"Just some buzzing. Weird feeling. I'm sure it's fine."*

I watch him with concern but don't respond.

*"Your friend should be held in one of the facilities in this section of the City,"* Alistair informs us. *"Check the ones that aren't two stories first."*

We're going along pretty well, unnoticed, strolling down the street like we live here. I broadcast, calling out in my mind specifically for Travis as we walk, in case he's nearby. There's no answer, but we haven't come across trouble either.

Of course, the moment I start to relax, my thoughts come back to jinx me.

"Halt!"

We do no such thing. We keep walking. Quickly.

"Halt!" the female voice commands again.

Alistair curses under his breath, then slowly turns around. We follow suit, having no other instructions.

Before us stands a stocky woman with an olive complexion and intelligent gray eyes that remind me of Nora. Her visible skin bears several faded scars, and her raven hair catches in the wind, the feathery strands fluttering around her head in a black halo. In her hand is a large bladed weapon. Behind her are a few uniformed young adults.

I drop the MindSpeak thread, my focus creeping from my ability to a rising panic.

Thomas gulps, and with my thread forgotten, he whispers, "Who's the scary lady with the axe?"

"The Axe," Alistair hisses back.

"That's what I said."

"No, that's her name," he mutters. "Makes you wonder why she carries it around, huh?"

"Not funny," Cali mumbles, stepping backward, her eyes wide.

Alistair angles his chin at the woman, his jaw set. I can feel my pulse quicken and thrum in my throat.

"What's with the faces?" the Axe asks, her stance casual. "Did I scare you?"

We all decide not to answer.

The Axe tosses her weapon from hand to hand, walking toward us. "Now, it seems I've caught myself a fine group of intruders. If you come with me peacefully now, we can avoid conflict."

Alistair turns his head slightly in our direction. "All of you run. I'll hold her off. But you need to get as far away as possible. Find your friend. Get back to the tunnel. No matter what happens to me, don't stop."

"We're not leaving you!" Thomas gasps.

"Wait just one minute," the Axe calls leisurely. "Did you say *tunnel*?"

Alistair's onyx eyes flick back over to her, a warning in his glare.

The Axe glances at us, then growls, "I see." She turns to the soldiers behind her. "Go to the seal."

She reaches to press some sort of panel in her wrist, but before she can, Alistair makes a wild sweeping motion with his arm, indicating we book it out of there. Cali grabs my sleeve, pulling me back, then turns and pushes Thomas into a run. We bolt down the street together, our boots sliding on the icy road.

The ground rumbles as we trip over ourselves, dashing madly away. I manage to look back without stumbling to my knees, to search for Alistair with my eyes.

I get vertigo just looking at him, like my head is dropping but my shoulders are pulling in the opposite direction. Alistair still looks the same, only a vortex replaces where his chest should be. It swirls together with his figure. Shadows seem to be sucked toward him while also radiating out. His sandy hair waves around his face like he's caught in a whirlwind, and the light seems to bend around his form, turning the already dull atmosphere color-deficient.

Aside from the void in him, flashes of light and not-light dance over his arms. Fractures trace his skin, reminding me of a cracked plate. The energy surrounding and enveloping him radiates in waves, pushing and pulling like the tides at the port.

The Axe squares her shoulders, says something incomprehensible and then charges at Alistair. He stays silent, despite the growl of the shaking earth and the crackling thunder overhead, and stands his ground. Craters crack in the pavement under his feet from an impossible amount of pressure.

We round the corner, and the standoff disappears. A heavy screech sounds behind us, and I swear I see a flash of lightning strike out of the corner of my eye.

"What the heck is that?" I pant as Cali pulls me along.

"No idea!" she replies. "But we need to find Travis and get out of here!"

"Over there?" Thomas suggests, pointing to a gray brick building that's shorter than the others. "He said to look in the one-story buildings."

"Sure," I say as we turn, now weaving through the narrow alleys in the direction of that building.

Even though we run our hardest, with the ground shaking and the odd turns, we're only a few blocks away from Alistair, and definitely not "as far as possible."

We all flinch at the sound of an explosion. Sirens wail throughout the streets. Some distance away, a lot of people are screaming in a mass panic.

*We've gone and done it,* I think to myself. *We messed up.*

Another explosion. More lightning. Screaming. Smoke.

*Alistair,* I plead weakly as we dash down the narrow alley. *What are you doing?*

# Chapter XXXII

## —Travis—

## Lockdown

Everything is going according to plan.

I wake up rejuvenated, alive, ready to get back out into the world held together by the black and white nature of war as well as the gray areas that proved not everything is as it seems. I feel energetic, impatient.

Isaiah greets me just after dawn as if everything is okay and I don't have an execution scheduled. It's four hours until the first rally of the day, the signal for our departure.

"I'll be out for a bit to take care of something," he tells me. "I'll be back later. Don't go anywhere. If someone catches you, you'll be in big trouble, and so will I."

"Right."

With that, he is gone.

I take a hasty yet refreshing shower, running the plan again and again through my head, then checking and double checking my belongings, waiting for the bell.

And then it chimes, the effervescent chord calling the citizens to participate in a patriotic singalong, some news updates, and the general torture that is standing for an impossibly long time while officials ramble on. I haven't been to any rallies, but HG's told me enough about them through our notes.

I leave Isaiah's flat without looking back, not allowing even a hint of remorse to cloud my judgment, because for better or worse, I'm going to get out, and I'm going to be free.

HG is already at the checkpoint, hiding in the cool shadow of the nearest two-story building. I jog over casually, hoping I don't look suspicious. Nodding at her, I pull my new coat tighter over my shoulders to keep out the clawing cold.

"So far so good," HG whispers. "Glad you could make it, Travis."

I snort in spite of myself.

"Come on." She motions with her head in the direction of the gate.

We walk together for a bit before pacing ourselves at intervals of five minutes apart. I wait for HG to disappear, holding my breath and then exhaling into the crisp morning air. After five minutes, I head the same way she went. And soon, we'll—

"Oh, hello there, Travis."

I wince inwardly. *No, no, no, no.*

"Not going to the rally, hm?" the Secretary says, her voice just barely holding an accusing tone. "The Yield is awfully lenient, especially at a time like this."

I try for a confused smile. "I'm busy. I see you're not going either?"

"I, too, am busy." She fixes me with a stare as frosty as the streets of Kaltic.

I shrug. "Right. Well, I'll see you around."

Her gaze hardens. "Why aren't you at the rally? Or at the Yield's, for that matter?"

"I believe I told you." I force a smile through gritted teeth. "I'm quite busy."

"With?"

I crack my neck. "I thought you would know, having tabs on everybody like you do."

Before she can open her mouth to reply, a thundering growl shakes the ground, followed by a piercing screech. I fail to mask my alarm. I reach for the indigo stone hidden under my sleeve.

"What was that?" I manage to ask, schooling my emotions to match the Secretary's.

She narrows her eyes. "Get inside a building. I will investigate."

More reverberating booms and explosions echo off the clean walls of the perfect city. I glance around, tense. Something isn't right. Thankfully, the Secretary dashes away, the rally dilemma forgotten for now. I use the distraction to my advantage and scramble around the corner to follow the mapped-out trail to where HG is waiting for me.

"Are you alright?" HG asks. "Did you hear that? Why are you late?"

"I was held up by the Secretary. As for the explosion, I have no idea."

HG doesn't answer. Her eyes lock onto something behind me. I turn.

A few blocks away smoke rises, black in the pale winter air. A crack of lightning crashes down, bringing with it the taste of metal and more smoke.

I take a futile step back from the direction of the calamity, trying to ignore the cries of people growing closer and the rattle of destruction coming nearer. From the side where the tunnel lies, just beyond the block we're standing on, rough explosions sound, and in the opposite direction, the panicked voices of the citizens rise in a loud hysteria. We're surrounded.

On my wrist, the indigo stone pulses and trembles, glowing through my coat brighter than before.

And then, from the direction of the disaster, three shapes run out of the smoke. In an instant, the stone is in my hand as a dagger.

"Stay back," I whisper to HG, whose face is a mixture of fear and curiosity.

"Travis?" a voice calls.

The world freezes. My eyes scan over their faces. Cali, Thomas, Jack—

"Jack?" I mutter incredulously as the figures fully emerge.

He peers at me, his hazel and gold eyes squinting, as if he can't really believe what he's seeing. Of course, neither can I.

"Travis!" Cali squeaks. She nudges Thomas and Jack. "Guys! Don't just stand there!"

Except we do, standing frozen, each side staring at the other.

"What are you doing here?" My words come out harsher than I intended.

"We came looking for you." Jack bridges the gap between us.

"How did you find me?"

"I'll—" He glances over his shoulder, back at the street they came from. "I'll explain later. Now that we found you, we need to get Alistair and get out of here."

"Who're they?" HG edges away from the newcomers suspiciously.

"Friends," I say.

Thomas nods. "Tova, Ezra, and Kappa are by the hole. Alistair's also a friend, but he's fighting this woman called the Axe back there."

I curse. “That’s not good. Were you guys the ones wrecking the city?”

“Alistair,” is all Jack says. Because that definitely makes sense.

“Right,” HG says, her mouth set into a grim line. “This is a touching reunion, but we really should be going now.”

“Okay, there’s a tunnel back that way we went through to get inside,” Jack says, glancing back again.

HG narrows her eyes. “It was sealed off, wasn’t it?”

“Yeah, we broke through,” he says. “But we need to get Alistair before we can go.”

His words buzz around my head along with the sirens in the background and the screaming.

“We need to be fast,” HG says after a moment. “They’re going to shut Kaltic down.”

Cali waves us forward, and we dash back the way they came. Near me, Jack closes his eyes, pausing briefly, then he skips back up to match our pace. We move closer to the alley with the drainage ditch, and to the carnage. Smoke billows out of caving buildings, and a few fires lick at the wooden rubble in the streets. Bodies of Kaltic soldiers are strewn about. I don’t dare look at their mutilated features as I forge ahead.

And then, there’s the Axe, her back to us. We move around a new crater in the street, then we all stop to watch the battle.

The Axe looks battered but far from defeated. She’s as lively as ever. A good few feet in front of her stands the most troubling thing I’ve glimpsed since the swirling indigo sky I see in my sleep.

I couldn’t describe it, what the man looks like, because the black hole isn’t a man, but it is. Just staring into the void makes me feel powerless, drained. The area surrounding the battlefield has lost its color, the world painted in grayscale.

Looking away from the man, I focus on the monotone buildings around us, reduced to piles of debris and rubble.

The Axe darts to the side and swings her weapon with reckless abandon, catching the man—the monster—in the shoulder, or so it seems. Before the blade touches him, it drops to the ground as if gravity decided to call on it. From the outside, it's like watching a warrior fight a powerful deity.

I glance back at my allies. HG stares wide-eyed at the scene. Cali is waving her arms about, and I notice pieces of wreckage flying off to the sides, piling up out of our way and theirs. Thomas is looking around nervously, and Jack's eyes are closed again.

*"Alistair."* Jack's ability rings out stridently, open to all.

Voices rise as the nearby citizens receive the message, crying for something they don't understand.

And then it happens all at once.

The ground beneath the monster's feet combusts, the Axe flies backward on some freak wind, Thomas shouts something about machines, and a strong voice calls out over the chaos.

"Alistair!"

Standing on the toppled wall of a building, a small figure holds out his hands.

His calm, soothing voice quiets all noise. "Alistair. Please stop."

Isaiah's honey-gold hair is windswept in the now harsh breeze. No one makes a sound except for Jack, who, upon seeing the Yield, squeaks and steps back. Isaiah hops down from his perch on the crumbling wall.

Alistair turns toward him, his icy and distant gaze meeting Isaiah's warm amber eyes. He's eerily calm as he walks to the monster, his movements all relaxed and casual, welcoming.

"I'll have to ask you to stop this," Isaiah says.

The Axe, who was buried in the wreckage after hitting the side of a building, struggles under the pile of debris.

Alistair's mouth forms a tight line, like he's unsure what he's doing and it's taking all his concentration to focus on Isaiah.

It's almost too quiet to make out, but above the whipping wind and the cracks of lightning comes the monster's whistling voice.

"We need to leave."

Isaiah narrows his eyes. "And you will; please calm down. We can negotiate this peacefully."

"Yield," the Axe groans. "You can't reason with him. Let me handle this."

Isaiah's gaze flicks over to her, his eyes burning with a sort of rage only someone as calm as him can possess. "Right. Because you're doing so well handling this. Like you're keeping my city safe and in one piece. Sure, go on, Axe, when you can stand up."

"Please do not argue." A new voice cuts through the tension.

Many pairs of eyes trail to the approaching figure. The Mind steps into the street, his trench coat billowing behind him. There's an object in his hand. He smiles, glancing at Isaiah.

"Don't worry, my friend, I won't let it happen like the last time," he says. "I've perfected the lockdown drill."

HG shouts a warning, but it's already too late.

The Mind presses the button.

# Chapter XXXIII

## —Jack—

## **Flight (Reprise)**

I can feel my own panic radiating off me, tumbling over the watching civilians, over my friends, over everything.

And then the man presses the button.

The panic stops. Everything stops. All the objects Cali has floating in the air drop. My MindSpeak cuts off mid-sentence. The lightning flashes are gone too, and the ground no longer trembles. The vortex's tug starts to ebb, leaving me both relieved and empty.

Alistair's strange form starts to dissipate. The glowing cracks in his skin seal back together, and the winds around him die. He collapses heavily onto his knees.

This area of the city is in ruins, reminding me painfully of my own city miles and miles away from here. But the reality of our situation brings me back quickly.

I'm so alone. My ability has been snuffed under whatever technology that man used. Without my MindSpeak, it's unnatural to think by myself. Even when I could control my broadcasting, I always knew a link to everyone else was there. I could always reach out. But isolated in my own mind, I feel trapped. I'm suffocating.

Drowning.

A hand rests on my shoulder, and I glance back at Thomas. Beyond words, emotions, and my ability, Thomas knows me so well that he doesn't need to be told in order to understand.

I smile, grateful for his reassurance. He places his other hand on Cali's shoulder. She's wiggling her fingers and staring at the nearest object as if she can't comprehend what just happened. Next to her, Travis gazes at his transparent palm.

*What—?*

There's no time to think. I break away from the group and sprint to Alistair, slumped on the ground, and grab his shoulders. The Axe has dug herself out from under the collapsed wall and is rolling to her knees. I'm not strong enough or tall enough to support Alistair, but I loop my arm around his back and stand my ground. Thomas darts over to us and helps me with Alistair on the other side. We turn together to face the man with the button.

He tilts his head, staring coldly at Alistair. "Welcome back to Kaltic. You will not get away as easily as you did a decade ago."

I hadn't noticed earlier because I was so focused on the nullification of my ability, but looking up, I see the walls looming higher than I thought. Only, they're growing. The walls push higher into the sky and then curve to cover the city like a dome. Shadows rise over us as lights on the underside of the dome flash on, illuminating the city. A huge sheet of metal blocks out the winter sun.

There's a grating noise as manhole covers pop off and metal spikes shoot up.

I whirl around, watching the spikes rise around us. A woman with a single key in her hand directs civilians into the nearest building, outside of our circle. Too shocked to move, we watch as the spikes launch tendrils at each other, connecting like a fence. Then they spark, sizzling bars of lightning that dance in between the wires.

"Electric walls," Thomas murmurs, staring at the new cage.

Now, all who stand inside the ring are my group, Travis and his friend, the Axe, the button man, and the blond man.

Oddly, Thomas doesn't seem fazed by any of this. He scans the faces of our opponents, glances at the dome, then the electric fence.

The friendly man's eyes widen at the new setup of "his" city. He gasps. "Mind, what did you—"

"Dear friend." The Mind's gaze is steely, analytical. "I fixed your memory process. Surely you know what is happening."

"Yield's files were busted?" the Axe says in disbelief.

The Mind fixes his icy eyes on Alistair once again. "Thanks to a certain force, yes. But that issue was addressed a few days ago, I believe."

Thomas tugs my sleeve, hissing, "Jack. While they're talking, I have an idea."

I don't pry my gaze away from the adults, but I tilt my head toward Thomas slightly, whispering back, "What is it?"

"My ability isn't gone. I'm not sure why, but we can use this to escape. I'll shut down Kaltic."

"How?" I ask.

He closes his eyes and shakes his head. "Just trust me. Please."

I think of all the times Thomas has put his unshaking faith in me. It'd only be fair to do the same for him.

"Okay," I whisper. "Okay. You do what you're going to do. Just be careful."

He gives me a tight smile. "Of course."

The Axe strides toward her colleagues, then turns to face us. Her piercing eyes hold a terrifying light, a roaring flame.

"Stand in a line," she commands, hefting her huge weapon. "Or he's first to feel the electric wall."

She points with the blade at Travis, who glares at her in turn.

"Do as she says," the girl with Travis says, motioning for Thomas, Cali, and me to stand beside them.

It all feels eerily familiar to our first run-in with the Indifferents, only we had Nora, and I've never seen Travis look so stressed. And we're not surrounded by people, but a sizzling barrier instead.

We all line up shoulder to shoulder, our backs to the fence.

"Set down your weapons, if you have any," the Axe instructs.

Cali lays down a couple of daggers. No one else in our group has anything. I look at Travis, who also possesses a stone, but his indigo eyes are focused on the ground and a bead of sweat trails down his temple, despite the cold.

"That includes your touched bracelets," the Mind says.

My eyes shoot involuntarily to the stone on my wrist. It's dull and devoid of its usual light. My throat goes dry, and I try to swallow, but it's too hard. Seeing the stone's light snuffed out is like the final nail in the coffin.

The machines not only took our abilities, but our hope.

"It doesn't come off," Travis says for both of us, his voice rough.

"I'm quite sure it does, Travis," the Mind replies.

Travis fidgets for a second, his translucent fingers twitching, before he crosses his arms and shakes his head.

"They don't come off. I just tried. They don't transform under your machines." Travis looks at me. "Right?"

"Yeah," I squeak. "S—Sorry, I guess."

"We can amputate your wrists for you, then," the Axe suggests, her face contorting into a wicked grin.

"No!" the Yield and I say at the same time.

Travis's shoulders are rigid as he says, "It's not like we can use them now anyway—they're ability based."

I give him a grateful look, but he doesn't tear his gaze away from the Kaltic leaders.

"Fine," the Axe relents, glancing at the Yield.

"Now, back to business," the Mind says. "You are all intruders, not counting HG-8057. The standard procedure for your kind is a trial, though I'm sure you will not have to stand before the Judge. The obvious charges stacked against you are the destruction of Kaltic, resistance and harming of city officials, mass murder, and kidnapping of citizens—"

"I'm not being kidnapped," the girl with Travis interjects boldly.

He pauses, frowning, before ignoring her. "Because at least two of you are touched, you can either be reclaimed or executed. Your choice."

The Axe smirks smugly. "No matter what, you are no match for the machines of Kaltic."

"What do you mean by 'reclaimed?'" Cali asks.

"You will return to my experiments," the Mind explains simply, his eyes shining with an intense, manic light. "There is more work to be done. How nice of Alistair, especially, to come back and bring more candidates as well. I can continue where I left off."

"That's … terrible," Cali says. "Why won't you just let us go?"

"Security reasons. Kaltic does well isolated, and if the outside world other than our trusted merchants were to know about us, our utopia would be destroyed."

"Where is the Light?" the girl next to Travis demands, her pale green eyes burning. "I wish to speak with my father!'

"He's—" the Yield begins before the Axe slaps her hand over his mouth.

"Don't try to buy time for your 'friends,'" the Axe sneers. "Time's up. Now they decide."

Thomas shifts next to me ever so slightly. I catch his eye with a look that says, *We need to talk*, and tap Cali, who sees my expression, nods, and nudges Travis.

We all share a split-second mental conversation, despite the loss of my ability.

"We haven't had time to talk it out as a group," Travis says. "At least grant us that."

The Axe squares her shoulders. "No. Why would I allow you to plot anything?"

*This isn't good.* A bead of cool sweat traces down my temple.

"W—Wait!" I say, holding up my hands and stepping forward. I kick Thomas in the foot with my heel as subtly as I can. "We can make a deal!"

The Axe cocks a skeptical eyebrow as Thomas turns ever so slightly toward the group.

"What are you talking about?" the Axe says, and while I'm sure the question is rhetorical, I answer anyway.

"A—A deal," I repeat, holding up my wrist and tapping the stone. "I'll give you this if you let us go."

The Mind leans forward, his eyes sparking with interest. "What about the stone Travis possesses?"

"You can have that too," I say quickly, surprising myself. "You can have the whole stone. You know, it's pure radiation that gives us our abilities. If—If you turn off your machines, we'll be able to take them off."

"You guys know the way to the tunnel?" Thomas asks behind my back, his voice so low I can barely hear him over my own.

The Axe is watching me suspiciously; the Mind is totally focused on my words. The Yield has his arms folded, his eyes on my friends behind me, but he doesn't say anything. I don't dwell on it. Instead I channel my best inner Nico to be as chatty as possible.

"If there's a hole in the wall," the girl mutters. "The Mind's barrier will cover it. But there's a gate nearby that's not sealed."

Thomas exhales. "Alright. I'll try to see what I can do about the gates. When I yell 'go,' everyone needs to run to that exit. Got it?"

I pause my rambling as the Mind calls the Yield over and talks into his ear. The Axe looks over to them, partly listening. Exhaling slowly, I keep my eyes trained on them while listening to my friends.

"What about you?" Cali whispers. "You're coming, right?"

Thomas pauses. "I—I can't guarantee that I …"

"Thomas, no," she says. "We need to all make it. We didn't come here just to lose another member." Then I hear her add, "Another family member."

He exhales. "Fine. Fine, okay. Just trust me. I trust all of you to do your part, and I promise I'll do mine and find you."

"What about the others at the tunnel?" Cali says. "Aren't Ezra, Tova, and Kappa still there on the inside?"

"They should be fine if they followed Alistair's instructions to run at the first sign of danger," Thomas answers. "But you can't go back."

"He's right," the girl hisses. "We can't take any detours."

"Can Alistair even move?" Cali whispers. "He looks kind of out of it."

"We'll help him," Travis says.

"Shut up!" the Axe exclaims to the Mind. "Try to look in the present for once instead of ranting about all your plans! Can't you see we still have a big problem on our hands, idiot? Those kids were whispering about something."

The Mind's gaze clouds over. "You … You're right. My apologies." His eyes focus back on me. "So, boy, was everything you told me a lie?"

"No! Of course not!" I wave my hands. "I swear the deal is legitimate!"

Thomas taps my back twice, then steps up to meet the Axe's eyes. His expression morphs from one of serious determination to an angry indignance.

"How dare you," he says, his voice full of rage. "You can't keep us here!"

"We can," the Mind says firmly.

Thomas steps back, shaking his head. "No, no I want to get out!"

The rest of us tense for his next move. I've never seen Thomas like this, so I'm not really sure what to expect. I just stare at him in shock; he always keeps a level head.

Thomas whips around on his heel and bolts toward the electric wall. The Yield screams at him to stop. Cali gasps. Alistair, having gained some consciousness, calls out to him, but he ignores it all.

Thomas rams his shoulder into one of the metal spikes jutting from the ground, roaring, "Go!"

The electric tendrils stop sparking and hissing, and everyone sprints forward. Travis helps support Alistair while Cali grabs my hand, dragging me through the space in the wires. The girl leaps through after us, then turns back to hold the metal lines open for the others before pushing us into the street.

Cali and I run side by side as the girl with Travis takes the lead.

I glance back at Thomas, who's wincing in clear pain, still shouting at us to go. My feet stop. I can't leave my best friend here.

Travis whirls around and grabs my wrist, yanking me forward and leaving me with no time to hesitate. The others are already ahead, so we're bringing up the rear with Alistair stumbling along with the girl's help now.

"Come on, Jack," he growls. "Thomas knows what he's doing."

Nodding tensely, I pick up my feet and dash after the others.

"After them!" the Mind yells, and I can hear the Axe's rough footsteps as she bolts through the wires.

We follow Travis's friend, weaving between buildings and dashing down the empty streets. More spikes shoot from the ground, but they aren't doing anything. A huge metal creature that resembles a horse with large spikes in its head launches in front of us. It bowls into a building, and the wall crumbles down on it. Silver glints off its dented back. It doesn't get up.

The buildings behind us have collapsed, shaking the ground as they fall. I faintly hear the Axe cursing as she's blocked by a wall of rubble.

Finally, we reach the gate and stutter to a stop. The walls around it are cracked, and the metal panel that I assume is the gate seems to be crushed between the walls on both sides.

"No…" the unnamed girl mutters, her pale green eyes wide.

"Travis!"

We duck as debris tumbles from overhead. Beside me, I see Travis tense up, turning to stare down one of the alleys that open up to the gate.

A boy around Travis's age is calling to him. His hair is mussed and there's a streak of blood painted down the side of his face.

"Travis!" he yells breathlessly, his arm out toward us. "The gate's destroyed! You can't get out through here!"

The rest of them turn, and Cali hisses something about not having enough time. The girl with Travis steps forward to the boy.

"What about the other gate?" she snaps.

"Still functional," he says, his breath halting. "I was posted at this gate. An earthquake destroyed part of it. It's just a useless wall."

Travis glances at the girl, then growls at the newcomer, "Why should we trust you?"

His blue eyes are wide and serious. "Because Kaltic is going down."

Travis's eyes narrow.

The boy exhales. "You told me about the outside world, Travis, and I didn't care because I thought it was safe here. But the outside world *is* here. It's come to us. I can't stay."

People are screaming from the buildings; their terrified voices accent the sirens and shouts of the Axe nearby.

Cursing, Travis turns to the rest of us. "Let's go. Follow AR."

I don't have time to question anything as the boy, AR, bolts down the street, us close at his heels. Alistair seems to have gained enough energy to run as well.

We dodge more monstrous machines and spikes, and finally skid to a stop outside the gate.

We advance toward it, not really sure what to do next. We'll have to act fast if we don't want the Axe to catch us. It's closed, but Thomas promised he'd figure it out.

And I trust him more than I trust myself.

But the gate, this giant metal panel in the wall, isn't moving.

*Please, Thomas,* I plead in my head.

*Fly,* is the response.

Pounding footsteps grow louder as they get closer. Suddenly, the gate begins to rise.

The moment it's open high enough for us to squeeze through, I shove Alistair out, then make sure Travis's allies go next.

"Come on!" I shout at Cali and Travis, not wanting to step fully through while they're still on the wrong side. But a group of soldiers have caught up, and two are locked in battle with my friends. And the gate has stopped rising, the gap only four feet high.

"Cali!" I shout. "Travis!"

Cali pushes her opponent away and runs to me as the gate starts to lurch back down in shuddering creaks.

She crouches and slides through, pulling me with her as I call for Travis.

He turns and sees the gate is only two feet open, and his eyes widen. He kicks the soldier away and scrambles to the gate.

One foot high.

He's one foot away.

The gate closes with a thundering *boom.*

Now, sitting in the snow, we all stare at the blank wall, silent.

Our mission to rescue Travis. *Is it for nothing?*

A ghost-like hand shoots through the wall, transparent fingers grasping at the air. By pure instinct, I reach out and grab it, tugging.

Somehow, his hand is solid in mine. I pull, believing with all my might that I can bring him through. Cali gets the idea and latches onto my arms. The others soon join our efforts. We fall backward when Travis tumbles through the wall, all of us crashing into the snow.

And for a second, we stare at each other as if we can't quite believe what just happened.

How we all just escaped.

How we're still missing two adults and a robot.

And how Thomas isn't with us.

# Chapter XXXIV

## —Travis—

## **Loss**

The back of my head throbs angrily. I can barely stand straight, but I yank Jack to his feet and help Cali up. Someone has to make sure we keep moving.

"W—Wait," Jack says shakily. "Thomas is still in there. And Kappa. A—And Tova, and Ezra. They could still be inside."

I grit my teeth. "We need to go. Now."

He doesn't look at me. Cali stifles a sob, pounding a fist into the wall.

Was it worth it? They've known Thomas longer than they've known me. If they came this far just for me, how far would they go for him? I know I'm not worth Thomas's sacrifice. The sacrifice of four others.

If only Jack got my message that I could handle things *by myself.* If only Alistair hadn't blown the place up. If only I was stronger, then I could have gotten out before this mess.

"Come *on,*" I urge, dragging Jack ahead of me and waving Cali to join us.

I bring up the rear of our group, making sure everyone moves at a fast pace despite the snow and sharp wind. Now that we're out of Kaltic and no longer restricted by whatever machines the Mind built, our abilities have come back.

I unfold the map and find our location according to where we came out. There's a port on this continent, through the mountains, but we're on foot, and we're going too slowly.

Jack's broadcasting nags at my already jumbled mind. I'm not sure if he knows he's doing it, but it's getting irritating real fast.

*"What will happen to Thomas?"* his worried thoughts scream. *"They'll kill him, won't they?"*

"Shut up," I growl. "Keep moving."

He looks at me, his eyes wide with shock. His hazel gaze is fractured and broken by the sudden loss, and I know my harsh tone isn't helping.

"Sorry," he whispers.

I exhale, blowing puffs of white in the chilly air. My wrist burns where the stone is missing.

I was the last one to make it out, and not under normal circumstances. I was too slow, and the gate closed while I was still on the wrong side. I remember looking at my hands—they were fading, an effect from being caught between the machines I assume—and shoving my fingers at the wall. I needed to get through.

I won't let another closed door stop me.

I remember hands finding mine on the other side and tugging. But the rest of my body wasn't able to fade, so it was like being pulled into a solid wall. I thought my hand was going to pop off. Then, the stone suddenly started to glow again, burning, searing my flesh. It caught on the wall, unable to go through. It had shattered then; I could feel the shards cascading down my wrist and to the ground.

That's gone too, lost in Kaltic. Bits and pieces of one of the most powerful weapons in one of the most powerful cities.

I don't want to bring up this loss yet. Not until we've made it out of the mountains. The going is hard though, since AR has to help support Alistair, and we don't have enough supplies for all of us. Not to mention the stinging cold that seeps through our clothes and boots, threatening us with frostbite.

Still, I push them as fast as I can.

Along the way, HG comments that Kaltic can't follow us, not for a few hours anyway, because of the full lockdown. The sun continues to climb in the sky as we trek through the white, and we don't stop for more than a couple of minutes at a time. I make sure of it.

"Travis," HG finally calls as we near the rocky shapes of the mountains that climb high into the sky. "We need to stop."

"Just a little farther," I urge.

"No, we're far enough away for now. We need to stop."

I rub my bare wrist. My aching legs agree with her logic, but I can't allow myself to give up now.

"We might be able to find a cave or something," Cali murmurs, and everyone nods in agreement.

"At least there isn't a blizzard," HG says, glancing at the grumpy clouds. "We have a bit of luck on our side."

"Don't say that," I mutter. "You'll jinx it."

"You must be tired," AR comments to HG, his tone casual and indifferent despite him doing the most work out here. I'm still shocked that he made the split-second decision to help us, though I know his reasons. He decided he had a better chance out here. Staring at the desolate and icy landscape, I'm not so sure.

"A little bit," HG answers. "I've gone pretty far, but I have never been able to make it past the mountains."

"That's not reassuring," he says under his breath.

"Don't worry," Cali says, her normally bright voice dull. "We've made it through before."

"Because of Kappa and Thomas," Jack mumbles.

HG glances back toward Kaltic, squinting. She shuffles ahead, her boots squeaking in the snow with each step. After a few minutes, the ground becomes noticeably rockier. HG turns around to face us, a little way away, by walls of craggy rock.

"Over here!" she calls, stopping outside a decent-sized cave.

We all stagger in, huddling away from the entrance and out of the wind.

Even though it's not the same one, the cave brings back memories of the beginning of this whole mess.

We gather near the end of the pocket, and HG builds a fire with the supplies she brought. I find myself regretting that I don't have my stone-lighter. Sitting in a circle around the fire, we refrain from any conversation and just listen to the harsh winds and the crackle of the flames.

"We could have helped him," Jack says, his voice quiet. "We should have all made it out."

Cali nudges his shoulder. "At least he has Kappa, right? She wouldn't leave without him. Thomas is smart; he'll be fine."

"He was wary of going on another journey to begin with," Jack whispers miserably. "I dragged him along. He should be at home right now."

"Jack …" Cali starts.

He looks up at her. "You should be at home, too. And Alistair. I can't believe— I shouldn't have—" He puts his head in his hands and runs his fingers through his hair. "I—I was so selfish asking you to go. And now Thomas is gone—"

*Smack.*

"Ow!" he yelps, rubbing his arm where Cali hit him.

"Calm down, you're making me nervous," she says. "Thomas is my friend, too. He asked you to have faith in him, didn't he? No one forced us on this journey with you. I jumped at the opportunity to leave. And I'll bet that if you didn't tell Thomas and just left camp without a word, he would have snuck out to find you anyway, regardless if he knew what you were up to or not.

"Because that's who Thomas is. He puts his full trust in you, and he expects you to trust him back. *So trust him!* He knows what he's doing. All the time. Thomas is so aware of himself and his surroundings that it's almost scary." She punches him in the arm again. "So stop—stop worrying. We'll find him again. Because heaven knows where you'd be without Thomas, the voice of reason. Where any of us would be, really."

Jack smiles weakly. "You're right."

"I'd like to apologize," a new voice speaks up.

All heads turn to Alistair, now sitting up and rubbing his neck.

"What for?" Cali asks.

He opens his eyes wearily. "You know. All the damage I did. I didn't mean for it to get out of hand. None of this would have happened if I—"

"Oh, not you now," Cali grumbles. "I don't care how old you are, I will slap you, too."

He holds up his hands. "I know, I know, I just feel I should take the most blame for losing him. I am here to make sure that kind of thing didn't happen. And Tova and Ezra are still there, too. God, I— We lost so many people."

"None of us could have predicted the outcome," Jack says somberly.

"Do you know if …" Alistair trails off, his dark eyes glued to the ground. "Can you tell if they're alright?"

Jack nods slowly, then winces. “No, I’m sorry. Their connection is blocked. I don’t … They must still be in Kaltic.”

“Idiots,” Alistair mutters. “I told them to get out if they heard anything go wrong. Don’t tell me Tova lied. I should have known—she never agrees with me.”

I don’t know who he’s talking about, but if Kappa’s with them, they’ll survive. She’s an Evil-engineered robot, after all. Besides Kaltic, the Evils have some of the most advanced technology in the world.

“I’m sure they’re fine,” I put in just for good measure. I know all too well the importance of bringing up the spirits of my comrades after a crushing defeat.

Alistair looks up at me, and something akin to recognition flashes across his face. “You look exactly like—”

“Travis.” HG taps me on the shoulder, tearing my attention away from him.

“Mhm?”

She points to the cave entrance where AR is keeping watch. His face doesn’t betray any emotion, but he’s tense, his eyes narrowed.

HG folds her arms. “Something’s coming.”

# Chapter XXXV

## —Jack—

## Greater

I have to hope Thomas will be alright, as will Tova and Ezra.

I try not to flash back to months ago when Nico was captured by Evils. My mind doesn't want to carry the burden of guilt for leaving someone behind in the clutches of dangerous people again.

Because Thomas is my best friend, everything is that much harder. I've known Thomas my entire life, and there's no way I can live without one of my only constants. So I have to hope and believe he'll be fine, for his sake, for my friends, and for me.

"Jack." Travis shakes my shoulder. I notice his indigo stone is gone. The only thing left is a painful-looking red mark on his wrist.

He looks different since I last saw him, which is no surprise. He's wearing less black—he has a warm brown coat, and the faded dye in his hair is so faint, it's hardly there. There are bags under his eyes, and his face is gaunt, tired.

"Hey, Jack," he repeats.

I blink. "Yes?"

"HG and AR say something is coming toward us," he says.

"Wait, who?"

He rubs his face. "The girl is HG. The guy is AR. They don't have names, just codes."

I commit those letters to memory. "Okay, so what did you need?"

"I said something is coming toward us," he answers. "I want your opinion. Should we move out or wait?"

I force my mind to process what he just said. Something's coming for us? And Travis wants *my* thoughts on our next plan of action? Not Alistair or Cali, who both seem to be thinking clearer than me at the moment, despite the people we've lost?

Travis reads my face and glances back at the rest of the group, then lowers his voice. "Look, Jack, we need your input. I get that you're grieving and all, but Thomas will make it. What Cali said earlier is true." He exhales. "I know I can trust your judgment."

I take a deep breath. "Well, thanks. How close is this 'something'?"

He steps back and turns to the mouth of the cave where HG and AR are conversing quietly. "Come on. We'll show you."

I rise, following him a few feet to the front. Cali lifts a questioning eyebrow but doesn't ask. Instead she turns to watch the fire.

We peer out into the white. Travis points. "There. That dot coming from the hillside across from us. It's moving pretty fast. We think we have about an hour before it reaches us, and it doesn't seem inclined to turn."

I squint, my eyes locking on the object in the distance, heading from the mountains. It *is* getting bigger.

"It did not come from Kaltic," AR adds, scratching his head.

Something stirs in my chest.

"Let's wait for it," I say slowly.

Travis's eyes narrow. "Okay."

"Are you sure—" HG begins, but Travis holds up his palm.

"I trust Jack's instincts," he says, glancing at me. "Besides, no one wants to go out there, not with the weather and evening approaching. If he thinks this is important, we can't afford to miss it."

My gut churns, and knowing I barely ate today, it's not because I'm about to be sick.

"I *know* this is important," I say suddenly, unsure where I'm finding the confidence.

AR shrugs. "I'll take your word for it. You're like a prophetic dream lord, correct?"

I raise my eyebrows, not sure if he's joking, because of his deadpan face. "Uh, sure."

Travis smirks. "I suppose we sit and wait, then."

So we do.

It's eerily quiet with only the crackling of the fire and the whistling wind outside the cave. I sit with Cali and Alistair by the fire, letting my mind wander away from reality. Travis and his friends wait at the entrance of the cave for our incoming visitor.

---

*"Travis?"*

The familiar voice calling Travis's name startles me fully awake.

"No way," I breathe, hopping up.

"Jack? Cali?"

I whip around to the entrance to see three new figures at the mouth of the cave. A tall girl with gray eyes, her face shadowed by a large puffy hood, stands next to a shorter companion, his warm maroon gaze surveying the scene. They're both dressed warmly, each carrying large bags on their backs. Behind them is a silver man, similar to Kappa—a sort of humanoid robot.

"Nora?" I say, not totally believing my eyes.

"Nora?" Travis echoes for good measure.

"And Cole," her partner pipes up, grinning.

"Nora!" Cali bounces up excitedly. "And Cole!"

Alistair looks to us, then at the new arrivals. "Nora Moreau."

She beams at him. "Ah, I remember you! The Captain, or something. We spoke a little after the battle, right? And before that, when you tied me up." She turns her attention to Travis. "Travis, what are you doing here?"

Travis shakes his head, a small smile forming. "I should be asking you the same thing."

She laughs. "Well, I got your message and then went to find Cole, who decided he wanted to disappear off the face of the earth for a bit. It was difficult, but I located him pretty fast, which is mostly his fault for telling me so much about his other projects. Anyway, we built Sigma over here"—she motions to the robot behind her—"and then we went to find you. There was no luck tracking you, so we went looking for Jack instead, in hopes that he'd have a better lead. And now we're here! Sigma travels very fast."

"How did you find me, though?" I ask. "I mean, the whole tracking part."

"I built a device that pinpoints the Potestatemium," Cole explains. "Or the stone, as you call it. We tried to find Travis's, since I'm told he has a part of it, but something was blocking the sensor. So we located yours and have been following your trail ever since."

"It was Kaltic blocking your connection," Travis says, clearing his throat. "The machines there block all sorts of ability-related things."

"That's why I couldn't reach you," I mutter.

"Speaking of Kaltic," HG butts in, "we should get out of here as soon as possible. The city is close, and it's dangerous."

"I've never heard of Kaltic," Cole says, tilting his head.

"It would make sense." HG nods. "The city is completely isolated from the outside world, aside from our coffee exports."

"Citizens of Kaltic don't even know there's anything out here," AR adds. "The city is all we've known, and it has been around for generations."

"Interesting," Cole says. "You'll have to elaborate this to me further. But I digress. If what you say is true, we must leave now."

"Can Sigma transform like Kappa?" Cali inquires.

"Yup!" Nora says proudly. "His design is based off Kappa's, and we may or may not have borrowed blueprints from both the Evils and Indifferents to build him."

"Cool," she replies.

Cole counts us under his breath, then turns to Sigma and relays instructions. Sigma nods, his face unchanging as he accepts orders. Then, plates in his arms, legs, and torso fold out, and more machinery pops out of hidden sockets as he transforms.

After five minutes of the metal rearranging itself, a huge machine sits before us. It's sleek in design, shaped almost like an arrow. Much like Kappa, long metal legs jut out from its sides like some sort of insect. The robot is much bigger than Kappa, though. Large enough that we can all fit inside.

Which is exactly what we do.

A panel in the side of the robot slides open, revealing a mostly hollow space with odd-looking seats lined up in rows.

Cole sighs. "I know it's not very conventional for now, but there are many of us, and I would rather not make anyone ride outside. It might be cramped, but try to make as much room inside as possible."

Nora smiles. "Come on, guys! It's warm in there." With that, she ducks into the robot, crawling up to one of the two seats at the front.

Cali shrugs and joins her, sitting in one of the middle rows, and the rest of us follow through. It's a tight fit with all of us pressed against each other, but no one complains because at least we're out of the cold and are safe, for now. Cole is the last one in. After checking a few things, he climbs over everyone to sit beside Nora. He presses a button on the console and the panel closes. It shimmers for a second, then the wall is transparent, like a window.

"Hey, Jack," Nora says, twisting around in her seat. Her voice is quiet. "Where's Thomas? And Kappa, for that matter."

I can feel the robot lift as it stands up while my spirits drop inside my stomach.

"He's in Kaltic," I mutter. "He sacrificed himself so we could escape. We lost Kappa and a couple of friends too. They're still in Kaltic, as well."

"Oh."

I don't mention that they could also very well be dead. Their connection is blocked, after all, but the last time we saw them was when we departed from the ditch. Whether they were caught, crushed, or have survived, I don't know.

I watch the window as Sigma bounds forward at a speed faster than Kappa.

"Shouldn't we go back for them?" Nora says.

"No," Travis answers. "It's too dangerous, and we only just got out. We don't have many supplies, and I doubt you and Cole have enough to last all of us."

"Where is it that we are going?" AR asks.

Cole sighs through his nose. "To the Indifferents. Travis is right; we do not have enough supplies, and we need to restock. If any of you are looking to end your journey, you can also join them. They are a safe organization that does not interfere in Good and Evil affairs."

"And they live in a city?" HG asks.

"No," Cole responds. "Our original base is in a giant building in the desert, though we have a second campus in another building inside an abandoned town."

"So, both 'camps' are situated in buildings?" AR muses. "Where do the people live?"

"The people stay in dorms or small rooms and live together as a community. Everyone eats at the same time in a big cafeteria, and most people work their own jobs to fulfill the needs of the camp."

"It's like Kaltic, then, but at the same time, it is very different," AR says.

Cole turns around, his eyebrows raised. "I'd imagine. Do tell me about Kaltic."

I listen as HG and AR take turns explaining their city, intrigued by the idea of the Important and the way everyone has a code instead of a name. Cole asks about the Important, and how they live for many generations without aging. It reminds me of Cole's ability to become almost immortal.

"They transfer souls," Travis says when neither HG nor AR have an answer for that.

"Where did you learn that?" HG asks.

"I spoke with the Mind and Isaiah—I mean, the Yield—and apparently their bodies are completely bionic. After a certain number of years they appoint 'pure' citizens to take their place when their souls take in too much information and die, I suppose. I have no idea *how* they do it, though," Travis explains.

"That would explain when my father went in for a trial to become the Light," HG murmurs. "He wasn't always the Light, but one day he was called in. I don't know of anyone else becoming an Important like that. As far as I know, the Light is the only position that changes so frequently. After that, he never was around much."

Cole scratches his head. "That seems like a very complicated process. It would make sense that no human can live forever …" He falters, his gaze wandering. "Well, it does sound interesting. Perhaps I can stop by Kaltic someday to find out exactly how they're doing this. It isn't natural in the very least, but it is a fascinating concept."

Nora coughs. "Let's hope the Evils, or the Goods for that matter, never find out about this. They already know about the stone. This new piece of information could start something even bigger than last time."

I shudder at the thought of Evils descending on the city of Kaltic, the peaceful and empty streets flooded with panicked citizens, much like they were today. As much as I find Kaltic dangerous and disturbing, I wouldn't wish war upon anyone. Knowing what the Evils are capable of with their terrible weapons and immoral ways, having Kaltic under that kind of threat doesn't bode well with me at all.

"Hey, Cole?" I pipe up.

He glances back. "What is it?"

"You know how you once told me about Travis's ability being perceived as a different element by the stone?"

"Yes."

"Do you think that has something to do with how he died and then vanished?"

Travis sits forward, listening to our conversation with interest.

"I think the stone did play a part," Cole muses. "I know from what you told me before that the stone shifts its user's consciousness to a separate space that allows them to see what the stone sees. Depending on his ability, it may have done that as he died. Only, it didn't just shift his consciousness, but his whole body. Though, this is only a speculation, and I'd need to do more research."

"Oh."

"Well." Nora stretches, yawning. "I'm going to take a nap. I suggest everyone tries to get some rest while we go through the water, as we'll be walking a bit after we get back on the coast. We'll make a few stops, but I don't want to run Sigma too hard, and we need to keep moving if we want to make it to the Indifferents before all of our supplies run out."

Cole nods. "Agreed."

Silence falls over the cabin. I watch through the window as the landscape blurs past. It blends into the rusty port scene and then we're launching into the waves, submerging underwater. The trip is a lot smoother and faster compared to Kappa, but I find myself wishing I had Thomas here to talk to. I want him to know we found Nora and Cole, and I know he would be ecstatic upon meeting Sigma. Most of all, I want him to be safe.

He has to be.

# Epilogue

## —Jack—

## **No Longer Indifferent**

It takes us far less time going back than it did getting to the mountains, though Cole keeps pausing the journey to make notes and collect data and whatnot. This can take hours sometimes, though Nora makes sure he keeps it brief. Without her intervention, we'd be stuck for days.

Upon our arrival at the Indifferents' main camp in the desert, Thala orders Cole straight to her office.

"She looks mad," Cali whispers to me as we watch the two of them leave.

The rest of us are sitting in the lobby. Thala has water and food sent our way, since she doesn't want us in the cafeteria where we could easily slip out and wander around.

Nora taps her fingernails on the outside of her cup nervously. "I hope they don't hold Cole for too long."

"Do you know why she was so angry?" Travis asks.

"Well he's really important to the Indifferents, as he's their inventor and their oldest member—"

Cali sputters out her drink. "He's their *what?*"

Alistair and Travis have a similar reaction, while HG and AR just glance at each other and nod like they've already accepted this as the norm. I guess the outside world really can't get any weirder than it has with everything they've seen over the past couple of days.

Nora sighs. "I guess you don't know. Cole was one of the first affected by the Evil radiation, and the effect it had on him turned him immortal, in a way. He ages extremely slowly. He's been around for a *long* time, guys. Oh, and he invented the stone. Anyway, he sort of just disappeared from the Indifferents, and that caused a bit of a panic within the facility. Actually, I hear he does that a lot, but they know he's plenty capable of taking care of himself, so the search didn't last very long. I doubt he'll be in much trouble; his disappearance was more inconvenient than anything, really. Anyway, I went to find him for help. He had been working on projects outside of the Indifferents secretly, and they did wonders to aid us in finding you as fast as we did. Projects like Sigma, which I helped him with, and the stone locator."

We all turn to look at Sigma, who is sitting on the floor with a paper and a pen, drawing.

Nora smiles. "They probably thought Cole was kidnapped or something. I'm sure Thala isn't too mad at him."

I chuckle. "Makes sense."

"Speaking of Cole and the stone," Nora begins. "Where's your stone?" She points to Travis. "Last I saw, you had one on your person the morning you 'died.' Jack gave it to you, very foolishly I might add. Did you lose it? Classic."

Travis rolls his eyes and glances at his wrist where the angry red marks stands out.

"Yeah, what happened to it?" I pipe up.

Nora sighs in exasperation before Travis can speak. "Seriously, Travis, you lost it didn't you? I mean, I always thought you were anal-retentive and disgustingly organized, but it turns out that isn't the case. I'm very disappointed in you, you know."

He blinks, his face contorting into an expression that falls somewhere between confused and offended. "Let me explain. I didn't lose it. You weren't there, but during the escape from Kaltic, everyone had to pull me through the wall. The stone used the last of its power to boost my ability, since it was blocked at the time, and it shattered as I faded through. The pieces are stuck in Kaltic."

Nora's face darkens. "Well … That's not good."

"Maybe Thomas can find them?" I mumble hopefully.

Nora shakes her head. "We'll get there when we get there."

"Nora." Sigma's unusually melodic voice drifts up in our silence.

Her attention switches quickly to the robot sitting crisscross on the floor, holding up the paper.

The ghost of a smile crosses his face, an eerie attempt at human emotion that reminds me painfully of Kappa. "Look what I drew, Nora."

She takes the paper, and her eyes sweep the page. "Wow, that's pretty neat, Sig."

Nora turns to me, holding the sketch up to my face. "Look, Jack, it's you."

I blink as I take the paper and stare at the pen lines. At first, it just looks very scribbly, but when I focus, I see it. All the hurried dashes on the page shape together to form a creepily realistic rendition of my face. I haven't seen myself recently, but I look tired in the drawing. Exhausted.

I hand the paper back to Nora. "That's neat. Your robot is an artist."

She grins. "We didn't program him like that. He just likes to draw. Faces, especially."

"Did I miss much?" Cole walks back in, trailed by Thala.

Nora glances up. "No, but Sigma made another drawing if you want to keep that. What's up?"

Cole scrambles to see the sketch while Thala stops in front of us and plants her hands on her hips.

"We've got news," she says all business-like. "A message was dropped during your absence, Jack."

"From …?" I inquire.

Thala's expression hardens. "The east. Evil headquarters. One of the Evil big shots sent a nice little note demanding we hand you over, or the Indifferents will be brought into the war. Of course, you were gone at the time and no one knew where you went. We answered them truthfully to avoid war, but now that you're back …"

Alistair stands up abruptly. "You're not turning him over." His voice drips venom.

Thala furrows her eyebrows. "Now—and let me finish—it wouldn't be our fault if Jack just … goes missing. You've already proven we can't control you, right? So, the only solution we could come up with in this short amount of time is that he disappears."

I gulp. "You're not going to kill me, are you?"

Thala rubs her temples. "What do you people take me for? No, we're not going to kill you. That defeats the whole purpose. Instead, we're going to have you run away. Stay gone until this whole thing blows over. Maybe they'll assume you died on your own or something. We can't know where you're going, but you always know where you can contact us. So, go to the most remote or unexpected area you can. Don't get caught."

"What about my family?" I ask.

She shakes her head. "You can take them with you if you'd like, but you'll have to make that decision soon."

"So, when do we leave?" Cali asks.

I note she says *we* and not *Jack*.

"As soon as possible," Cole answers. "I will take you back to one of my many laboratories if you have nowhere in mind to go."

Nora's eyes light up. "Oh, that would be great!"

Travis nods. "I know I'm going with you too, but what about them?" He tilts his head at HG, AR, and Alistair.

"Of course I'm coming," HG says indignantly.

"Me too," AR volunteers.

"Wait a second," Alistair says. "Why don't you just hide the stone somewhere? It's been that way for years, correct?"

Cole shakes his head. "The fact that Jack found it and Evils and Goods both tried to get to him before, means hiding it just won't work anymore."

"Then it's settled," I say finally. "I guess I'll disappear."

Thala nods. "Alright. We'll start packing supplies for you all. I'll make sure to send messages to Cole updating you all on what's going on out here once things settle down a bit."

Resigned, I say, "Got it."

With that, she turns on her heel and heads back the way she came.

Cole grins sheepishly. "Let's get you all situated for the night."

***

Now rested and fed, I lie in a bed in the Indifferents building. Cali and Nora are sleeping across the room in the only bunk bed. Travis sits at the desk by the window, his head resting in the crook of his elbow, propped up on the smooth wood surface. His friends are in the smaller room next door, while Alistair is off somewhere still speaking with Thala.

I recall him being quiet throughout the rest of the evening. He never did say he was coming with us either, and with a pang of guilt I remember his intent wasn't to return to the Indifferents, but it's my fault he has nowhere else to go, no friends left. Though he didn't seem defeated. More like something between determined and focused. I think whatever happens, he'll be alright.

For now, everything's as it should be. At least, that's what I want to believe. Except, there's a gap—a huge hole where it's clear something is missing.

Some*one* is missing.

"Hey, Travis?" I call, not sure if he's still awake.

He stirs in the chair, sitting up. "Yeah?"

"What was it like to live in Kaltic?"

He turns to look at me, his indigo eyes catching the moonlight from the window.

"If you're worried about Thomas," he says, his voice low, "don't be. I know one of the Important in Kaltic. He wouldn't let anything terrible happen to Thomas. I'm sure of it. So don't worry. Besides, the whole place is dependent on machines. Thomas'll be fine. He could probably take charge of Kaltic single-handedly if what he did before is anything to go by. The machines don't affect him like they affect us. Plus, he'll have Kappa to watch his back."

I exhale. "Yeah, I guess. I just— I've known Thomas my whole life, y'know?"

"I know exactly what you mean. Just trust him and go to sleep."

I shake my head. "Everyone's telling me to *trust*. But even you didn't trust us completely when you first met us, right?"

He snorts. “Of course not. You’re what, twelve? Besides, I didn’t know you or your friends. So, that’s completely different. But Nora was there, and I trusted her. The only person I have full faith in is Nora, but I grew up with her.”

“I’m *thirteen,* and I don’t think it’s the same.”

He cocks an eyebrow. “Isn’t it? You grew up with Thomas, right?”

“Well, yeah …”

“So, you know him. Let me guess—you know him so well that you could probably read his mind. And he understands you so well that he doesn’t need to depend on your ability to know what you’re thinking, either.”

“*Well*, yeah.”

“So, it’s not different in that case. I mean, I’m not saying to trust everyone you come across, duh. There are people out there who are two-faced, if you know what I’m saying. But you understand Thomas, and he puts enough faith in you that he’d follow you blindly, no matter what. Because he knows you’re a good person, Jack.” He sighs. “That can’t be said about all of us.”

I don’t answer that. Travis thinks I’m a good person? I’m selfish and dense, or at least that’s what my guilt tells me every time I fail someone, which has been awfully frequently over the past few months. But we all make mistakes, I guess. And Thomas is one of the smartest people I know.

I take a deep breath.

“You’re right,” I tell him. “He’ll be fine.”

Travis leans back and props his feet on the desk. “Of course he will. And we’ll go get him as soon as we’re ready. Now shut up and go to sleep.”

I smile. “Yeah. Goodnight, Travis.”

“’Night, Jack.”

I let my head fall back into the pillow. Even though my future is uncertain, and the futures of my friends are uncertain, I know everything will be alright. Because I trust my friends, my family.

And in a broken world like this, they're all I have left. This trust—it's all I have left. And that's all I need.

# Acknowledgments

To be quite honest, this second time around doing the marvelous thing most people know as "writing a book" (it's much more than that, really) was actually extremely difficult, at least compared to my first endeavor. Though *Indigo Fading* is twice as long, that's not the only thing that made it so hard, and along with all the new twists the year has had to offer, I'm surprised and pretty proud of myself that I was able to get it done.
Of course, I didn't do it all by myself.

First and foremost, I'd like to generally thank the people who've been supporting me through this entire journey, from family and friends, to teachers and influential adults who've guided me and led me to where I am today. I'd like to specially thank Sophia (I didn't forget you!), who offered her time and countless words of encouragement while I struggled through the editing process, often staying up with me well past two in the morning just to make sure I wasn't lonely. It means a lot.

I'd also like to give a huge thanks to all my betas, who saw the really rough parts of my manuscript way before I decided to flip everything on its head. Thank you to Christopher Bellotti and Kerri Beckman for taking the time to go through the craziness and make notes for me. Thank you to Talulah Ruger for reading through and giving me feedback. And thank you to Zarina and Kai for stepping up, despite the hectic school environment, to look at my manuscript and make comments (you guys are the best, love y'all). I don't know what I'd do without everyone being there for the nitty gritty parts, and I know for sure none of my work would have ever survived editing if not for these first beta runs.

Next, I want to thank my social media/marketing manager, Elena Clancy, who directs all the stuff I'd rather not do, being the social recluse that I am (I admit I'm afraid of the internet). Thank you for putting together my social media pages together with my project manager, Lilibeth Giles (hello, Mother, I love you very much), and promoting my work.

I'd also like to thank my cover artist, T.M. Franklin, for creating such an awesome cover! I love it to bits, and it really brings out the vibe I was going for with my story.

And now a giant extra-large thank you to my editor, Linda Hill, for not only beta-reading the manuscript, but also being flexible with my finicky working hours, coaching and encouraging me every step of the way, and giving me lots of insight on how to make my work better. None of this would be here without the work you've put in, so thank you, thank you, thank you.

Lastly, I'd like to thank my family for continuing to push me to keep going, even when the writer's block hits, even when the quarantine burnout hits, even when I go slightly kooky from time to time after being locked up in the house a tad bit too long. Thank you for putting up with me, and for helping me through this. I couldn't do it without you.

Finally, I'd like to give all the glory to God for sustaining me every step of the way. Only heaven knows I would have crashed and crumbled long ago.

And for all who came to the end of this book, thank you for reading!

## About the Author

Casey Giles is a teenage author who resides with her family in Houston, Texas. She's an artist and violinist, and she enjoys fine arts and learning about weird pieces of history. INDIGO FADING is the sequel to her debut novel, INDIFFERENTS.


**Connect with Casey at:**
Email: boodledoodle11@gmail.com
Instagram: @teenauthor_cg
Facebook: @CaseyAuthorIndifferents
Website: www.caseygiles.com

Made in the USA
Coppell, TX
22 October 2023

23218636R00166